MEATSMITH

MEATSMITH

HOME COOKING FOR FRIENDS AND FAMILY

ANDREW McCONNELL
TROY WHEELER

Photography by Mark Roper

Hardie Grant

BOOKS

CONTENTS

HOW TO USE THIS BOOK

We created Meatsmith with the home cook in mind. This book has the same focus. It's a book about a butcher and it includes meat in many recipes, but it's not a book about butchery. There are a heap of good books for those who want to take it a step further and master the skills of breaking down a whole beast. Here we're sharing different kinds of knowledge.

Australian butcher shops have always been social places; they are places of knowledge as much as they are places to buy produce and ingredients. At Meatsmith, we've noticed that when someone buys a steak, they first ask what it is, then how much it is and the next question is: how do I cook it? That exchange of knowledge is a constant in the butcher shop environment and that makes recipes a constant in our daily life. It made sense to us to document and evolve those recipes and create a record of how and what we like to cook at home.

What you will notice in this cookbook is that meat is not the hero ingredient in every recipe. Sometimes it's just there as a seasoning or textural element with vegetables or grains or salads doing most of the heavy lifting. This reflects the way we like to eat, and the way more and more people are incorporating meat into their home cooking: using better-quality meat in smaller quantities, for both everyday meals and special occasions. We've created a loose sort of template, a modern, rounded, balanced approach to integrating meat into your cooking, whether it's as a bit player or the star attraction.

Another feature of our cookbook is that there are more recipes in it than are listed in the table of contents. There are recipes within recipes – for dressings, condiments, sauces, marinades – that can be used in other contexts. Together these things can constitute a cooking arsenal of pantry and fridge staples that can be applied in many different ways to many different ingredients. Experiment a bit, mix and match, create your own flavours.

This is a book that contains something for all home cooks. There are quick, easy, accessible recipes you can cook every day and there are celebration and occasion recipes for when you have more time to roll up your sleeves and spend the day in the kitchen, pulling something amazing together for family and friends.

It's the way we like to cook at home. We hope you do too.

– Troy and Andrew

NOTES ON MEAT CUTS

All over the world there are many different names for the same cut of meat – we have endeavoured to provide clarification where needed. Different cultures use the same cuts for different cooking methods. There is no right or wrong, but it is important to understand how the piece of meat will react to different cooking methods. This way you will always get the best outcome.

The breakdown of an animal also differs between cultures, and often it is tailored to the type of cuisine. Even though the cuts are the same, each cuisine uses different parts to add flavour and texture to dishes.

A good butcher plays a big part in helping you find the right cut of meat to suit the type of dish you would like to cook – so don't be afraid to ask for guidance.

MEATSMITH

An introduction by Troy Wheeler

Andrew and I actually met in a butcher shop. He'd recently moved into the same neighbourhood as the shop I was managing and was out food shopping with his kids. I was interested in the Melbourne restaurant scene and so knew who Andrew was. I was a fan of his work. His restaurants, such as Cumulus Inc., Supernormal and Cutler & Co., seemed to have a particularly Melbourne style that spoke to me. We struck up a conversation over the counter that first day and whenever he came into the shop after that, or if I ate in one of his restaurants, we'd continue the chat about food, cooking and butchery.

One day, Andrew told me he was putting a dry-ageing room into his pub, Builders Arms Hotel, and asked if I'd come in to share some butchery skills and my experience assessing and grading meat with him and his staff. I jumped at the chance. I'd wanted to experience the inner workings of a restaurant for a while so it seemed like the perfect opportunity to tick that box. I felt I could offer something while also learning about how restaurants work, plus I'd get to meet, connect and talk food with like-minded people – all reasons why I'd moved to Melbourne in the first place.

I grew up in a small country town, left school at 15 and did my apprenticeship in the town's family-run butcher shop. It was a hard job but I loved it. I loved the direct feedback and the sense of building a rapport with the community; making products that people take home and who then come back to you, saying: 'that was amazing – what else have you got?'

I also became fascinated by how different meat would have different flavours and textures, depending on the breed of the animal, where they were raised or the food they ate.

The meat we generally sold in the butcher came from an abattoir, so we had no information about its provenance or breed but, as country butchers, we often processed whole animals farmers had raised themselves for their own

consumption. It was while working with these animals that I began to notice there were distinct differences between cattle from different properties. The meat from cattle that spent time grazing in an orchard, for example, tasted different to meat from animals that grazed exclusively on pasture. Different breeds presented different attributes of flavour and texture. I wanted to learn more, and to do that I needed to move to Melbourne.

I lined up some work at a butcher in the city, said my farewells, packed everything up and drove to Melbourne on a Saturday morning. When I rocked up to check that everything was good for me to start at the butcher on Monday, the guy who'd promised me the job told me there was no work for me after all. I was gutted but, as it turned out, it was one of those turning-point moments that life can throw your way.

I'd heard from a friend about a butcher called Peter Bouchier. He'd had a good experience working there so, immediately after being told I didn't have a job, I headed straight there to ask for work. Peter didn't have anything for me, but he must have seen something in me and offered me a position regardless. I started the following Monday and worked for him for the next 13 years, until I left to open Meatsmith.

At this stage of my life I was a simple country kid who hardly cooked. I wasn't really into food – it was mostly about fuel. I didn't drink wine either, only beer. But Peter and his wife Sue would take me out for dinner and I began to warm to the idea of restaurants and learning about – and enjoying – wine.

My eyes were also opened by the customers who frequented Peter's shop. Many of them were well-travelled people who ate out all the time. They'd tell me about the restaurants they'd gone to and what they'd eaten. Hospo industry people (Andrew being one of them) shopped there too and we had several regulars who were food writers.

These customers all contributed to my education; passing on cooking tips and food knowledge, telling me about dishes they'd eaten on a recent trip to Italy or local producers who were growing amazing mushrooms or making great cheese. It really started something.

I began researching, buying cookbooks, doing some cooking myself and going out to restaurants all the time. I went overseas and visited butcher shops and markets and restaurants, all the while soaking up as much information as I could. It became a passion. I certainly was given the opportunity to develop as a butcher while working for Peter but what I'm really grateful to him for was how he helped instil in me an ethos about and a love for food that's guided me to where I am today.

Any early conversations I had with Andrew about opening a butcher shop were all about me doing my own thing. But it was more hypothetical than a reality. I was comfortable where I was, well paid and treated respectfully, and the work I was doing with Andrew at Builders Arms was like a fun side hustle. But it also opened my eyes to other possibilities and, the more I thought about it, the more it made me realise I wanted to give it a crack. I came to realise that I didn't want to regret not trying it.

Andrew, a chef and restaurateur, had never thought about opening a butcher shop. But while talking about the possibility of me opening my own business, we came to recognise that we worked well together, and possessed complementary skills and similar ideas about what we thought a butcher shop could and should be.

The first conversations about Meatsmith started not just from a shared passion for quality, provenance and the art of real butchery, but in the lessons we'd learned along the way in our separate careers. Though we came at it from different angles as a butcher and a chef, we shared the same ethos.

We believed in having close relationships with the people whose produce we would be stocking, the farmers and producers who shared similar values to ours around ethical animal husbandry and working with rare breeds.

We wanted to source meat grown as close as possible to the shop and would always take animal miles into consideration, only working with farmers who could minimise the distance from the farm to the abattoir, reducing the stress on the animals caused by transport and processing.

We'd also pay close attention to breeds, choosing animals that have the genetics and attributes that allow them to thrive in the conditions where they're being raised.

We decided early on that if we couldn't access meat that met our criteria, we wouldn't stock it.

When it came to the actual shop, the overarching idea with Meatsmith was for it to provide all the essentials necessary for creating a good meal. It was never meant to be an emporium but we'd have everything – from wine and condiments to potatoes and garlic, even a few knives, some quality cookware and gadgets like meat thermometers – so that if you dashed in at the last minute after you'd forgotten that you'd asked people over for dinner, you'd still be able to pull together something impressive. This would be regardless of whether people were looking for something quick and easy early in the week (our chicken schnitzels and lasagne are consistently among our best sellers) or they came to buy something more ambitious like game birds or goat meat or pig's trotters to impress at a weekend dinner party.

What Meatsmith is ultimately about is making life easier for the home cook, whether they're novices or experts. It's sharing the knowledge we've picked up along the way that helps makes eating and drinking at home so enjoyable. That approach is reflected in this book. We wanted to share the relaxed way we like to approach cooking and entertaining when we're not on the job. And, just like in our butcher shops, we want to share information with the people in our community – cooking tips, shortcuts, how to make a burger that won't fall apart and end up in your lap. I discovered my passion for food in a butcher shop and from there learned to truly love cooking for family and friends. This book is a way to share that.

MEATSMITH

OPEN DAILY
MON. TO FRI. 9AM – 7PM
SAT. 9AM – 6PM
SUN. 10AM – 5PM

MEATSMITH.COM.AU

HOSPITALITY

An introduction by Andrew McConnell

Mention hospitality, and many people, particularly those like me who work in the industry, immediately think restaurants. Opening Meatsmith reminded me that hospitality can be many things. As much about attitude as industry, hospitality is about conversations and community, exchanging information and ideas, as well as feeding and watering people well.

It's also about helping people feel better about themselves, whether that's having friends over for a leisurely summer lunch in the backyard or pulling out all the stops with dinner in a restaurant. Hospitality's definitely part of your local butcher shop too; all those conversations about quick-fix solutions for weeknight dinners or ideas for what to cook for that big family gathering on the weekend.

I'd always been fascinated by the art of butchery but until Troy and I struck up a friendship and he worked with us at Builders Arms Hotel, it had never even crossed my mind that I would open a butcher shop. Once we started that conversation though, we began to see that by bringing our different skills, backgrounds and experience to the project – his in butchery and retail, mine in restaurants – there was the opportunity to create something really interesting.

A third element also came into play once we discovered the similar way we both like to cook and entertain friends and family at home. The professional skills Troy and I brought to the table were vital to the structure of Meatsmith but it was this third more personal element that really came to inform how we wanted the shop to function: as a valuable resource for the home cook.

We wanted the shop to be a place where you could explore and that would unfold the more you got to know it. We never intended Meatsmith to be a one-stop shop but, the way it panned out, it has the convenience of one if you're in a bit of a rush. It can help fill the gaps and I suppose there's a level of hospitality in that; the convenience of it. You can obviously buy meat but there are also pantry staples and wine. We also decided to stock certain knives we loved and our favourite pans and grills. In the beginning it felt kind of self-indulgent, throwing all the things we personally like to cook with and to eat and drink into our own shop. But the more we looked at it, the more it felt like the right destination.

In our early discussions, Troy and I talked about the traditional butcher shops of Europe, particularly in France; the kinds of shops that are part of people's daily routine and so also a part of the community. They are places you could talk cuts of meat or about roasting a chicken, or just bemoan the bad weather.

The timeless quality of those traditional European butchers led us to some non-negotiable criteria when we began looking for a retail space that would ensure Meatsmith would become part of its community. According to this 'manifesto', the space had to be in a high-density area, walking distance from a supermarket, close to a greengrocer, bakery and preferably a few other complementary stores like a fishmonger or a deli. It might seem like we were being neurotically specific but the idea of being part of the community was vital to the kind of business we wanted to run.

This was reflected in the design of Meatsmith, not just in the use of marble, terrazzo and timber that echoed the European style we admired, but in the way we wanted to display things in the fridges and on the shelves. With Lucinda and Matthew from Herbert & Mason architects, we designed our own display fridges. Unlike traditional high butcher counters that create a barrier between the customer and the butcher, our version had customers looking down into the cabinet, like in a jewellery store. This has created a friendlier dynamic in the shop, enabling us to have a better connection with our customers that encourages dialogue and makes the shopping experience more social.

We also brought a high level of customer service to Meatsmith that is directly informed by my restaurants. Then there are all the extras we make in-house that are based on recipes we use in the restaurants – marinades, dressings, pickles, vinaigrettes, sauces, jus, stocks – foundation, building-block recipes that allow our customers to achieve quality experiences at home.

Some people are suspicious of such shortcuts. It's the idea that they're somehow 'cheating' if you don't make them yourself. But, when you work in restaurants and are used to cooking something quick for yourself late at night after work, you become expert in the shortcut that doesn't compromise quality. We do a slow-cooked lamb shoulder at Meatsmith based on a dish that's been on the menu at Cumulus Inc.

since it opened. You can take that home, slide it into the oven for half an hour and you've got a perfect 8-hour slow-cooked lamb shoulder. That's a direct inside industry hack right there. We even encourage our customers to claim they did it all themselves.

Why not? It's hospitable to make things smoother, easier, better. And we live to make it easy for the home cook, to help connect the dots and to supply the knowledge, experience and confidence – as well as product and recipes – to make your experience at home the best it can be. The art of hospitality. It's what we do at Meatsmith and it's what we hope you get from this book too. Enjoy, and never be shy to take a shortcut if it gets you to the same (or a better) place.

WEEKNIGHT WINNERS
+ FLANK & GOCHUJANG BIBIMBAP
+ PORK SCOTCH EGGS
+ LAMB KOFTA FLATBREADS
+ THAI CHICKEN THIGHS & ZESTY SLAW

EASY ENTERTAINING
+ PERFECT PORCHETTA
+ HEAT & SERVE LAMB SHOULDER
+ STELLAR RIBEYES & T-BONES

MEATSMITH HERITAGE BUTCHER
FOLLOW US ON INSTA AT MEATSMITH

QUALITY MEATS

SKILLED BUTCHERY
—
CURATED WINE
SELECTION

SIGN UP FOR THE NEWSLETTER AT MEATSMITH

TO

Mortadella skewers with pine syrup

SERVES 2

20 thin slices mortadella
50 ml (3½ fl oz) olive oil
100 ml (3½ fl oz) pine syrup (see Glossary, page 247), or maple syrup
cornichons, to serve (optional)

The trick here is to grill the mortadella quickly, whether over charcoal or in a frying pan, so it gets slightly crisp, caramelised edges with a warm, soft centre. Pine syrup is a sweet and herbaceous Italian condiment typically served with cheese but it also works beautifully with this classic Italian deli meat. We stock pine syrup at Meatsmith, and some good delis and specialty food stores will sell it. If pine syrup is unavailable, the best-quality maple syrup you can find is a good substitute.

Preheat the barbecue to medium-high heat. Fold the mortadella slices into quarters, making a square parcel. Take 4 skewers and thread 5 of the folded parcels onto each skewer.

Brush the mortadella with the olive oil and cook for 4–5 minutes, turning frequently to make sure they get an even caramelisation. Just before they have finished cooking, remove from the barbecue, brush with a little pine syrup and return to the barbecue to caramelise. When golden, remove immediately.

Dress the skewers with a little more pine syrup to serve.

Prosciutto and persimmon

SERVES 4

1 persimmon (a crisp, non-astringent variety),
  peeled and cut into wedges
1 teaspoon extra-virgin olive oil
pinch of salt
10 slices prosciutto

This is a play on the classic Italian fruit and meat combo. It may sound obvious, but remember that the quality of a dish like this all comes down to the quality of the produce. Persimmon has a small seasonal window in late summer/early autumn, so timing is everything.

Combine the persimmon, olive oil and salt in a small bowl and toss to combine. Arrange the prosciutto on a platter, top with the persimmon pieces and serve.

Roast chicken rillettes

SERVES 4

size 16 (1.6 kg/3½ lb) chicken
4 tablespoons olive oil
1 large onion, finely diced
6 garlic cloves, finely chopped
1 celery stalk, finely diced
2 carrots, finely diced
250 ml (8½ fl oz/1 cup) white wine
1.5 litres (51 fl oz/6 cups) chicken stock
80 g (2¾ oz) flat-leaf (Italian) parsley
4 sprigs tarragon
4 bay leaves
8 sprigs thyme
100 g (3½ oz) duck fat
30 g (1 oz) chives
salt and pepper, to season
toasted bread crisps, to serve

In France, rillettes have regional variances with a wide range of ingredients and textures. Some have a fine texture, while others are coarser, and somewhat rustic. Our preference is a mixture of both.

Preheat the oven to 200°C (390°F).

Take the chicken out of the fridge and drizzle with half the olive oil and season with salt and pepper. Place the prepared chicken in a roasting tray and cook for 50 minutes. Set aside to cool.

Meanwhile, prepare the base liquid. Heat a large heavy-based saucepan over a medium heat. Add the remaining olive oil, onion, garlic, celery and carrot and sauté for 5 minutes, or until soft and aromatic. Season lightly with salt. Add the wine to the pan and continue to cook until the liquid is reduced by half.

Add the chicken stock, parsley, half the tarragon, the bay leaves and 2 sprigs of the thyme.

Increase heat to medium-high and cook until the liquid has reduced by three-quarters (or until you have approximately 500 ml/17 fl oz/2 cups of liquid remaining). Strain the liquid into another saucepan and add the duck fat, stirring until it is dissolved. Set aside to cool.

While the liquid is cooling, remove the skin from the chicken, trying to keep it in the largest pieces possible. Pull the meat off the carcass, shred and place in a large bowl.

Place the skin in one layer on a baking tray and roast for 10 minutes at 200°C (390°F), or until it is dry and crispy. Take care not to burn or overcook the skin. Set aside to drain on paper towel.

Season the meat with salt and pepper and finely chop the chives and remaining tarragon and thyme. Add the herbs to the meat and mix to combine. Add stock mixture and mix until combined.

Place the roasted chicken skin in a mortar and pestle and grind until it forms a rough crumb. Fold it through the mixture and season to taste.

Line a loaf tin or medium-sized ramekin with baking paper, leaving enough to overhang the edges. Place the mixture in the tin and fold overhanging edges in to cover. Refrigerate for at least 6 hours or overnight until set.

To remove the rillettes from the mould, pull the sides of the baking paper and turn the rillettes out onto a cutting board. It can be enjoyed immediately (otherwise, place in a sealed container and refrigerate for up to 1 week).

The rillettes are best served at room temperature.

Coal-roasted oysters
with bacon and devilled vinaigrette

SERVES 4

4 rashers smoked bacon, diced
12 large unopened Pacific oysters
1 tablespoon chopped chives

DEVILLED VINAIGRETTE
50 ml (1¾ fl oz) chardonnay vinegar
100 ml (3½ fl oz) extra-virgin olive oil
1 teaspoon dijon mustard
½ teaspoon yellow mustard seeds
pinch of cayenne pepper
1 teaspoon salt
½ teaspoon ground fennel
2 teaspoons brown sugar

The visual and sensory overload of grilling oysters over coals is almost as exciting and delicious as eating the final product.

Prepare your fire (page 103) or preheat a barbecue or grill.

To make the devilled vinaigrette
Whisk all the ingredients in a bowl until the brown sugar is dissolved.

To dress and cook the oysters
Cook the bacon in a frying pan over a high heat, gently stirring from time to time, until golden and crisp. Transfer to a plate lined with paper towel to drain excess oil.

When your fire or grill is ready, place the oysters flat-side facing up, balancing over and among the coals. Alternatively, you could place a grill rack directly on the coals and cook the oysters on this. Cook oysters for 2–3 minutes or until they start to steam and hiss and eventually pop open (remove each one at a time with a pair of tongs as they open). While the oysters are hot, remove the lid. Tip out half of the juice from each oyster and top with 2 teaspoons of the devilled vinaigrette, a pinch of crisp bacon and a pinch of chopped chives.

Pâté en croûte

MAKES 2, SERVES 24

PASTRY

500 g (1 lb 2 oz) plain (all-purpose) flour
10 g (¼ oz) salt
20 g (¾ oz) sugar
350 g (12½ oz) unsalted butter, diced and softened
1 egg
85 ml (2½ fl oz) water

MADEIRA JELLY

100 ml (3½ fl oz) water
6 titanium-strength gelatine leaves
250 ml (8½ fl oz/1 cup) Dry Madeira
2 tablespoons maple syrup
1 teaspoon white wine vinegar

PÂTÉ MAISON TERRINE MIX

10 g (¼ oz) chopped thyme
1 kg (2 lb 3 oz) minced (ground) pork shoulder
14 g (½ oz) salt
10 g (¼ oz) Espelette pepper (see Glossary, page 247)
¼ teaspoon saltpetre (see Glossary, page 247)
5 g (⅛ oz) ground white pepper
200 g (7 oz) chicken liver, roughly chopped
50 ml (1¾ fl oz) brandy
100 g (3½ oz) diced pork back fat (½ cm/¼ in diced)
100 g (3½ oz) porcini mushrooms, soaked, drained and chopped

Pâté en croûte is always a showstopper. Wheeling it out at Christmas and slicing into the pastry exterior at the table to reveal the layers inside is a truly satisfying experience. Be careful though – people may want you to make it an annual event for the rest of eternity. If you're good with that then you need to invest in some pâté en croûte moulds. They're quite specific to making this product. You can find them at good cookware stores or at an online charcuterie specialist store. We use two moulds for this recipe, each measuring 30 cm (1 ft/12 in) long × 10 cm (4 in) wide.

To make the pastry

Place flour, salt and sugar in the bowl of a stand mixer fitted with the paddle attachment. Add the butter and mix on slow speed until the mixture starts to resemble chunky breadcrumbs. Combine the egg and water in a separate small bowl. Reduce speed to low and slowly stream the egg mixture into the flour mixture until just incorporated – it is really important not to overwork the mix. If needed, tip onto a clean work surface and finish by bringing together by hand. Divide the dough into two equal portions. Flatten into rectangle shapes, wrap in a damp tea (dish) towel and refrigerate for at least 1 hour, or until needed.

To make the Madeira jelly

Combine water and gelatine leaves in a small bowl and set aside for about 15 minutes. Place the remaining ingredients in a saucepan over a medium heat, add the gelatine mixture and bring to the boil. As it just starts to boil, remove from the heat and set aside to cool. The jelly can be kept in an airtight container in the fridge for up to 1 month. Before using again, if it has been refrigerated, heat for 1 minute in the microwave so it can be easily applied.

To make the terrine mix

Add all ingredients to the bowl of a stand mixer fitted with the paddle attachment and mix on a medium speed for about 5 minutes. Remove the bowl from the stand mixer and work the mixture with your hands until it becomes tacky. Place in the fridge until you are ready to use.

TO ASSEMBLE
vegetable oil spray, for greasing
2 egg yolks, lightly beaten

TO SERVE
cornichons and mustard

To assemble the pâté en croûte

Spray the moulds liberally with oil. Roll one portion of the pastry out on a lightly floured surface into a large sheet about 5 mm (¼ in) thick. Place a mould in the centre of your pastry sheet. Using your mould as a template, trace out the shape of the mould on the pastry, turning it on each side so you can trace around it, and making sure you leave enough pastry for the lid. Using a small paring knife, cut out the pastry and line the moulds. Use your fingers to smooth over the pastry in the corners of the mould and make sure you push the pastry into the edges and corners so that the pastry is firm against the mould. Fill to the top with terrine mix, pressing the mixture down firmly to avoid air bubbles. Cut the pastry lids then drape over moulds, cutting to fit and pressing the sides with a fork to seal.

Use the smallest circle cutter or the paring knife to cut 3 vents about the size of a 10-cent piece in the top of the terrines. Brush with egg yolk. Return to the fridge for at least 1 hour. Using a paring knife, mark some decorative patterns into the top, such as diamonds or a herringbone, taking care not to cut through the pastry. Repeat the process to make the second terrine. When you are ready to cook, preheat the oven to 220°C (430°F).

Place the terrines in the middle of the oven and cook for 10 minutes. Reduce the temperature to 180°C (360°F) and cook for a further 15 minutes. Reduce the temperature again to 150°C (300°F) and cook for a further 15 minutes. Reduce the temperature again to 100°C (215°F) and cook until the internal temperature reaches 64°C (150°F), about 8–10 minutes.

Remove from the oven, allow to cool, and refrigerate overnight to completely set.

Ensure your Madeira jelly is warm. Slowly pour the warm jelly into the 3 vents in each of your terrines, pausing to let the liquid make its way around the edges. Once full, return to the fridge for around 1 hour, or until the jelly is cooled and set.

Remove from the moulds. Slice and serve with cornichons and mustard.

Chopped livers

SERVES 4

5 eggs
3 tablespoons Schmaltz (page 106) or
    unsalted butter
1 large red onion, finely diced
400 g (14 oz) chicken livers, trimmed of any
    visible fat or sinew
2 tablespoons dry Sherry
1 teaspoon thyme leaves
1 teaspoon Sherry vinegar
salt and cracked black pepper, to season
toasted sourdough bread, to serve

The famous Jewish saying: 'what am I, chopped liver?' is an expression of being underappreciated or ignored on a social level. It might be a reference to the fact that chopped liver is usually served as a side course rather than the main event. No guarantees, but this chopped liver recipe may put you back on the path to being the centre of attention.

Bring a small saucepan of water to the boil, lower the eggs into the water using a slotted spoon. Let cook for 6 minutes, then remove 2 eggs, (now soft boiled) and chill in iced water, peel and set aside. Continue to cook the remaining eggs for another 4 minutes (until hard boiled). When ready, remove from the water and chill, peel and roughly chop.

Melt half the schmaltz or butter in a frying pan over a medium heat, then add the onion and cook for 6–8 minutes until soft and starting to brown. Transfer to a bowl and set aside.

Season the livers with a pinch of salt. Melt the remaining schmaltz in a frying pan over a high heat, then add the livers and cook, turning occasionally, for 3–4 minutes or until well browned on the outside but still a little pink on the inside. Add the Sherry and thyme and shake the livers around the pan as the liquid bubbles and emulsifies with the butter. Transfer the livers to a bowl to cool slightly.

When cool enough to handle, transfer the livers to a chopping board and coarsely chop. Add the chopped liver and chopped hard-boiled egg to the onion and mix well. Season with Sherry vinegar and salt and pepper to taste. We like to serve it on toasted sourdough with the halved soft-boiled eggs.

Garden pickles

MAKES APPROX. 4 × 500 ML (17 FL OZ) JARS

6 serrano chillies
2 red capsicum (bell peppers)
1 celery stalk
1 carrot
½ head cauliflower, stems removed
130 g (4½ oz/½ cup) salt
3 garlic cloves
2½ teaspoons dried oregano
1 teaspoon red pepper flakes
½ teaspoon celery seeds
¼ teaspoon ground black pepper
300 ml (8½ fl oz /1 cup) white vinegar
300 ml (8½ fl oz /1 cup) canola oil

This is an Italian-style giardiniera recipe that works with whatever is in season and in surplus in your neck of the woods. So, if you are being overwhelmed by a tsunami of zucchini or broccoli or celery, you can use this one recipe for all those excess vegetables. The pickles last at least 6 months and they develop and change in flavour and texture over time. If you like a crisper pickle, best to eat yours sooner rather than later.

To make the garden pickles

Thinly slice the serrano chillies. Chop the red capsicum, celery stalk, carrot and cauliflower into 1–2 cm (⅓–¾ in) dice. Place the sliced chilli and chopped vegetables in a large bowl. Sprinkle on the salt and mix until well combined.

Place in a large container and pour in enough water to cover the vegetables. Seal tightly with a lid and refrigerate for at least 12 hours. Drain the water and rinse the vegetables under cold water to remove some of the excess salt.

Thinly slice the garlic, and combine in a small bowl along with the oregano, red pepper flakes, celery seeds and ground black pepper. Add the vinegar and stir until combined. Slowly whisk in the oil.

Divide the salted vegetables among sterilised jars, packing down with the back of a spoon, and top with the oil and vinegar mixture.

The pickles will be ready to eat after around 4 hours or will keep stored in a dark, dry place for at least 6 months.

To first sterilise the jars

To sterilise the jars, fill a stockpot or large saucepan three-quarters full with water and bring to the boil over a high heat, allowing to boil for 15 minutes. Reduce the heat to low and carefully place the jars into the boiling water. Depending on how many jars you have, this might be done over a few batches.

Once you have placed as many jars as will fit into the pot of hot water, turn the heat up to high again and bring it to a gentle simmer. Once simmering, leave for 15 minutes. Carefully remove the jars from the water and set aside on a tea (dish) towel to dry. Repeat the process if you have more jars than will fit in the pot.

HOW TO MAKE STEAK TARTARE

It is a truth universally acknowledged that a Frenchman in a nicely cut suit will add sophistication to any experience. We see that truth firsthand whenever Gimlet restaurant manager Samy Mir-Beghin prepares steak tartare tableside.

Samy studied the technique of tableside gueridon service in France. He now has created his own version and executes steak tartare tableside at Gimlet. The style and flair he brings to the process is very much France's loss and our gain. Samy elevates the process of emulsifying egg yolk with dijon mustard and olive oil, the timing of the mixing of the beef (at least two minutes to develop the right texture), and the meticulous shaping with a stainless-steel ring, into a realm somewhere between alchemy and performance art.

Like all good art, Gimlet's steak tartare is limited edition. We serve our tableside tartare at lunchtime on weekdays only, with a set number of portions per day – our contribution to the CBD hustle and bustle. We serve it with fries, slices of grilled baguette and a vinaigrette-dressed butter lettuce salad, so it's the perfect classic weekday power lunch dish, really. But it's also brilliant to serve your guests at a dinner party, particularly if you want to add a little theatre.

Our head chef at Gimlet, Colin Mainds, is also a fan of the tableside tartare and, with some input from us, he and Samy came up with the right balance of texture and flavour. Most of our ingredients are stalwarts of classic steak tartare but we believe the flavours should be big and bold, so we don't hold back on Tabasco, cornichons, capers, Worcestershire or chives (because, really, there can never be too many chives). We do add a few drops of lemon juice to bring a subtle flash of acidity to the mix and top the meat with a couple of excellent anchovies but, those few modifications aside, we stick to the script.

Obviously we pay strict attention to the quality of the beef. With steak tartare, the texture of the meat is important, so all our steak tartare is hand cut (grinding or mincing makes it too paste-like). We use rump cap or flank because it has much better texture than something like eye fillet. As an added bonus, it also has more flavour than eye fillet.

Please try this at home. And for some pointers on how to do tartare with style and flair, we'll let Samy show you how it's done.

Steak tartare

SERVES 2

200 g (7 oz) beef rump or striploin
6 cornichons
A small handful of flat-leaf (Italian) parsley
1 tablespoon salted capers, rinsed
1 small golden shallot
1 tablespoon dijon mustard
1 egg yolk
1 teaspoon Worcestershire sauce
50 ml (1¾ fl oz) light olive oil
1 teaspoon tomato sauce (ketchup)
1 teaspoon lemon juice
salt and freshly ground black pepper, to taste
Tabasco sauce, to taste
2 anchovy fillets
chives, finely chopped, to serve

TO SERVE
sliced baguette
French fries

Dice the rump into 3 mm (⅛ in) pieces and place in a mixing bowl. Set aside in the fridge.

Finely dice the cornichons, parsley, capers and shallot (this may seem torturous but the more uniform the size of the dice, the more refined the mouthfeel of the tartare).

Combine the mustard, egg yolk and Worcestershire sauce in a small bowl. Season with a little salt and black pepper. Using a small whisk, vigorously whisk while drizzling the oil into the bowl to emulsify.

Add the beef and, using a spoon, stir vigorously to combine. Continue to beat for 2 minutes to develop the texture.

Add cornichon, parsley, capers and shallot and mix to combine. Adjust the seasoning to taste with salt, black pepper, tomato sauce, lemon juice and Tabasco. Place a stainless-steel ring onto a serving plate and spoon in the tartare mixture, spreading it evenly. Carefully remove the stainless-steel ring, then garnish with the finely chopped chives and lay the anchovies on top. Serve with sliced baguette and French fries.

SOMETHING

CASUAL

Cheeseburger

SERVES 6

BEEF PATTIES
350 g (12½ oz) coarsely minced (ground)
    short rib
350 g (12½ oz) coarsely minced (ground)
    chuck beef
350 g (12½ oz) coarsely minced (ground)
    dry-aged beef rib cap
100 g (3½ oz) frozen beef bone marrow, grated

STEWED ONIONS
2 tablespoons olive oil
4 onions, sliced
10 g (¼ oz) salt
2 tablespoons unsalted butter
60 ml (2 fl oz/¼ cup) Sherry vinegar

TO SERVE
4 tablespoons clarified butter or olive oil
6 slices pre-sliced orange American cheese
6 potato buns or brioche buns, split
Kewpie mayonnaise
6 tablespoons Burger sauce (see below)
shoestring fries and dill pickles
salt and pepper, to season

BURGER SAUCE

MAKES APPROX. 400 G (14 OZ) / 430 ML
(13½ FL OZ)

This keeps for a week, refrigerated – use
it as dressing for a green salad or in a
ham sandwich.

250 g (9 oz/1 cup) Kewpie mayonnaise
50 g (1¾ oz) cornichons, finely chopped
60 ml (2 fl oz/¼ cup) tomato sauce (ketchup)
50 g (1¾ oz) American mustard
1½ teaspoon garlic powder
1¼ teaspoons onion powder
1¼ teaspoons ruby red paprika
½ teaspoons smoked paprika
pinch of cayenne pepper
1¼ teaspoons ground white pepper
½ teaspoon sugar
1 teaspoon salt

Whisk together the mayonnaise, cornichons,
tomato sauce and mustard. In a separate bowl,
whisk together the remaining dry ingredients,
then add the wet ingredients and continue to
whisk until combined.

This burger is unashamedly based on a fast-food chain burger, but without all the additives. Still, there's something great about occasionally treating yourself to something that's not exactly healthy. We like to use potato rolls – they're like sweet puffs of nothing but are great at soaking up the burger juices (so they end up in your mouth rather than on your clothes). We also like using American cheese, which doesn't add much flavour-wise but helps glue the whole thing together and gives the burger structural integrity. The trade-off? We use quality meat in the patty – a blend of short rib, chuck and rib cap, plus a little bone marrow. The stewed onions are not essential but do come highly recommended.

To prepare the patties

Combine meat and bone marrow in a large bowl. Using your hands, mix for about 2 minutes. Divide the mixture into 6 roughly 200 g (8 oz) portions and shape into patties. Set aside.

To make the stewed onions

Heat the olive oil in a stockpot or large saucepan over a medium heat. Add the onion and salt and cook for 5 minutes, stirring frequently until the onions begin to turn translucent. Add the butter and cook for a further 10 minutes, stirring every few minutes. The colour should start to become a bit darker at this point. Add the Sherry vinegar and cook until the liquid has reduced by half. Reduce heat to low and cook for a further 15 minutes. If you find that the onions are catching on the base of the pot, just add a splash of water to loosen them up a little. Remove from the heat and set aside to cool.

To cook the patties and assemble your burgers

Heat 2 tablespoons of the clarified butter or olive oil in a large heavy-based frying pan over a high heat until hot. Add 3 of the patties to the pan, pressing each one down with a spatula to flatten to about 2 cm (¾ in) thick and a diameter equal to your bun size. Season with a good pinch of sea salt and a little pepper. Cook for about 3 minutes, then flip and cook for a further 4 minutes. Remove from the pan, top each with a slice of cheese and transfer to a tray to keep warm. Rinse the pan, then repeat to cook remaining patties.

Once you have cooked the burgers, rinse the frying pan again and place over a medium heat. Brush each cut-side of the buns generously with mayonnaise, then toast, cut-side down, in the pan until deep golden brown.

Place 1 patty on each bun base and top with 2 tablespoons of the stewed onions (if using), 1 tablespoon of the burger sauce and the bun top. Serve immediately with shoestring fries and a wedge of dill pickle.

Vitello tonnato

SERVES 4

VEAL
1 tablespoon olive oil
1 kg (2 lb 3 oz) boneless veal loin
1 large onion, diced
2 celery stalks, diced
1 large carrot, peeled and diced
4 garlic cloves, sliced
200 ml (7 fl oz) white wine
2 tablespoons white wine vinegar
1 litre (34 fl oz/4 cups) veal stock

TUNA MAYONNAISE
2 large egg yolks
3 anchovy fillets, chopped
1 tablespoon dijon mustard
juice of ½ lemon
75 ml (4½ fl oz) extra-virgin olive oil
½ tablespoon salted capers, rinsed
250 g (9 oz) tinned tuna in oil, broken up
salt, to season

FRIED CAPERS
1 tablespoon olive oil
1 tablespoon salted capers, rinsed and dried

salt and cracked black pepper, to season

There seems to be a particular nostalgia to vitello tonnato that evokes a specific time and place for many people. Note that this dish is best prepared a day in advance to allow the liquid to set on the thin slices of veal.

To cook the veal

Heat the olive oil in a heavy based saucepan over a medium heat, add the veal and cook for 4–5 minutes, turning frequently to brown on all sides. Remove the veal from the pan and set aside.

Add the onion, celery, carrot and garlic to the saucepan and cook for about 5 minutes, or until soft. Add the white wine and white wine vinegar and cook until the liquid is reduced by half. Add the veal stock and return the veal to the saucepan. Reduce heat to low and poach for 15 minutes, turning often. Remove the veal and set aside to cool slightly before wrapping tightly in plastic wrap and transferring to the fridge to cool completely.

Continue cooking the poaching liquid for about 30 minutes, until the liquid has reduced by three-quarters (to yield approx. 250 ml/8½ fl oz/1 cup). Once the liquid has reduced, strain and set aside to cool.

Once the meat has completely cooled, remove from the fridge and slice very thinly. Spoon a little of the reduced poaching liquid over the base of a deep platter. Arrange the veal on the platter and top with 4 tablespoons of the reduced poaching liquid. Repeat layering with remaining veal and sauce. Refrigerate for 4 hours to allow the sliced veal to set.

To prepare the tuna mayonnaise

Ahead of serving, make the tuna mayonnaise. Place the egg yolks, anchovies, mustard, lemon juice and half the olive oil, capers and a pinch of salt in a large bowl. Using a stick blender, blend the eggs, slowly adding the remaining olive oil, until the sauce becomes the consistency of mayonnaise. Once emulsified, add the tuna and blend until smooth. Place the sauce in an airtight container and keep in the fridge until ready to serve.

To make the fried capers and serve

Heat the olive oil in a frying pan over a medium-high heat. Once hot, add the capers and fry until golden and crispy, about 2–3 minutes. Using a slotted spoon, transfer to paper towel to drain, then finely chop.

To serve, top the veal with tuna mayonnaise, crispy capers and salt and cracked black pepper to taste.

Glazed pork ribs with eggplant

SERVES 4

BRAISED RIBS

2 litres (68 fl oz/8 cups) water

375 ml (12½ fl oz/1⅓ cups) soy sauce

375 ml (12½ fl oz/1⅓ cups) Shaoxing rice wine

3 garlic cloves, crushed

1.5 cm (½ in) piece fresh ginger, finely sliced

3 spring onions (scallions), white parts only, finely chopped

80 g (2¾ oz) rock sugar (see Glossary, page 247)

1 cassia bark stick

2 star anise

2 kg (4 lb 6 oz) pork baby back ribs

PORK SAUCE

1 tablespoon vegetable oil

5 mm (¼ in) piece fresh ginger, finely chopped

1 garlic clove, finely chopped

75 ml (2½ fl oz) black rice vinegar (see Glossary, page 247)

75 ml (2½ fl oz) light soy sauce

10 ml (¼ fl oz) dark soy sauce

75 g (2¾ oz) caster (superfine) sugar

20 ml (¾ fl oz) sesame oil

60 ml (2 fl oz/¼ cup) chicken stock

TO SERVE

4 long thin (Japanese) eggplants

2 tablespoons grapeseed oil

7 g (¼ oz/¼ cup) coriander (cilantro) leaves

steamed white rice (optional)

Sticky, delicious goodness that must be eaten with your fingers. Team with a side of steamed rice, if you like. For the best result, braise the ribs the day before and leave in the braising liquid in the fridge overnight.

To make the braised ribs

Put all the ingredients except the ribs in a large stainless steel saucepan. Bring to a simmer over a medium heat, then reduce heat to low and cook gently for 15 minutes. Add the ribs and simmer for about 1½ hours, or until fork tender but not falling off the bone. Leave the ribs to cool in the braising liquid then transfer to the fridge until ready to use.

To make the pork sauce

Heat the oil in a wok or frying pan over a high heat. Fry the ginger and garlic until fragrant, then reduce the heat to medium and add the remaining ingredients. Simmer for 2 minutes then set aside.

To serve

Preheat the oven to 190°C (375°F). Remove the ribs from the braising liquid and pat dry. Cut the ribs into pairs, then coat with the pork sauce. Arrange on a baking tray and place in the oven. Cook for 20–30 minutes, turning every 5 minutes, or until hot and glazed.

Meanwhile, cut each eggplant in half lengthways and slice into 4 cm (1½ in) pieces. Toss the eggplant in the grapeseed oil and pan-fry over a medium heat for about 8–10 minutes or until cooked and golden. Transfer to a serving platter.

Stack the ribs on the platter alongside the eggplant, spooning over any excess pork sauce. Scatter the coriander leaves around the platter and serve with steamed white rice, if using.

Fried chicken sandwich

SERVES 6

BRINED CHICKEN
600 ml (20½ fl oz) buttermilk
4 eggs, whisked
50 g (1¾ oz) table salt
10 g (¼ oz) smoked paprika
10 g (¼ oz) ground black pepper
10 g (¼ oz) ground cumin
10 g (¼ oz) ground fennel
6 large (approximately 250 g/9 oz each) skin-on
    boneless chicken thighs

SEASONED FLOUR
200 g (7 oz) plain (all-purpose) flour
150 g (5½ oz) cornflour (corn starch)
17 g (½ oz) baking powder
17 g (½ oz) table salt
15 g (½ oz) smoked paprika
15 g (½ oz) ground black pepper
15 g (½ oz) ground cumin
15 g (½ oz) ground fennel

CHICKEN GLAZE
60 ml (2 fl oz/¼ cup) water
75 g (2¾ oz) caster (superfine) sugar
100 g (3½ oz) glucose
50 ml (2 oz) Tabasco sauce
50 ml (2¾ oz) soy sauce
2 teaspoons maple syrup or pine syrup
    (see Glossary, page 247)
pinch of fennel pollen (see Glossary, page 247)
    or fennel seeds

TO SERVE
1 litre (34 fl oz/4 cups) vegetable or canola oil,
    for deep-frying
6 burger buns, split
assorted dill pickles, sliced
1 quantity Ranch dressing (page 243)

Versions of this iconic sandwich are ridiculously popular all over the world and this is one of our bestsellers at Meatsmith. Do not forgo brining the chicken in buttermilk. It ensures you get the right ratio of soft and juicy at the core to the exterior's crunchiness. Oh, and pay attention to your bun – soft and sweet is best (we like to use potato rolls). For this recipe, you will need to prepare your chicken one day in advance.

To make the brined chicken

To brine the chicken, combine the buttermilk, egg, salt and spices in a large container with a lid. Add the chicken, making sure it is completely submerged. Close or cover the container and set aside in the fridge for at least 6 hours or overnight.

In the meantime, you can prepare the other components in advance.

To make the seasoned flour
Combine all the ingredients together in a large bowl.

To make the chicken glaze
Heat the water, sugar and glucose in a saucepan over a low heat, stirring, until sugar has dissolved. Remove from the heat and mix in the remaining ingredients, then set aside to cool. The glaze can be kept in the fridge for up to 1 month.

To cook the chicken and assemble the sandwich

Heat the vegetable or canola oil in a large heavy-based saucepan until the temperature reaches 170°C (325°F) or until a cube of bread dropped into the oil turns brown in 15 seconds.

Preheat the oven to 180°C (360°F) and place the seasoned flour in a bowl.

Working in batches, remove 3 pieces of chicken from the brine, shaking off any excess, then coat in the seasoned flour, pushing down to cover completely. Add to pan and deep-fry for 5–8 minutes or until the internal temperature of the chicken reaches 70°C (160°F). Transfer to a wire rack to cool. Repeat with remaining chicken, allowing the oil to reheat to 170°C (325°F) each time.

Toast the buns in the oven for a few minutes. Brush the fried chicken with the chicken glaze. Place 4–5 slices of pickle on the base of each bun and top with a piece of fried chicken. Drizzle 1 tablespoon of ranch dressing onto the fried chicken and top with the lid. Serve immediately.

Mussel salad with cucumber and 'nduja

SERVES 4

1 kg (2 lb 3 oz) mussels, cleaned,
    debearded and rinsed
60 ml (2 fl oz/¼ cup) dry white wine
100 g (3½ oz) 'nduja
2 thick slices sourdough bread
1 tablespoon extra-virgin olive oil
1 tablespoon white wine vinegar
1 tablespoon lemon juice
6 small cucumbers (Qukes), sliced
1 tablespoon shredded mint
1 tablespoon shredded dill
4 tablespoons Aioli (page 243)
4 tablespoons Lovage Oil (see below)

LOVAGE OIL

MAKES 80 ML (2½ FL OZ/⅓ CUP)

50 g (1¾ oz) lovage leaves (see Glossary,
    page 247)
80 ml (2½ fl oz/⅓ cup) grapeseed oil

Blanch the lovage leaves for 1 minute in a
saucepan of salted boiling water and refresh in
a bowl of iced water. Squeeze out excess water,
then roughly chop and pound the lovage leaves
in a mortar and pestle, slowly adding the oil.
Alternatively you could blend with the oil using
a stick blender in a small container.

Once the oil is a bright green colour, strain
through a fine sieve or muslin cloth and store
in the fridge until you are ready to use.

We first started serving a version of this dish at Marion and
it has evolved over the years. To this day it's still one of our
favourite ways to eat mussels. And, obviously, 'nduja makes
everything better.

Preheat the oven to 180°C (360°F).

Heat a stockpot or large saucepan over a high heat. Add mussels and
white wine, cover with a lid and cook for 2–3 minutes, or until the mussels
open. Drain, reserving the mussel juice, and set aside to cool.

Remove the mussels from the shells, discarding any unopened mussels,
and check again for beards. Strain the mussel juice through a sieve and
pour over the mussels. The mussels can keep for a few days stored like
this in an airtight container in the fridge.

Remove the skin from the 'nduja, break into small pieces and cook in a
saucepan over medium heat until the oil releases and the 'nduja is lightly
coloured and aromatic. Drain and set aside on paper towel to cool to
room temperature.

Remove crusts from the bread and cut each slice of bread in half. Coat each
slice in the olive oil and place on a baking tray lined with baking paper.
Bake in the oven until crispy and golden brown.

To serve, strain the mussels from the juice, reserving the juice, and place
mussels in a bowl. Dress with four tablespoons of the reserved mussel
juice, vinegar and lemon juice.

Add the cucumber and herbs and toss to combine. Place 1 slice of toasted
bread on each of 4 serving plates or bowls. Spoon a tablespoon of the aioli
onto each piece of bread and top each with the mussels, dressing and
cucumber salad. Drizzle each plate with 1 tablespoon of the lovage oil
and sprinkle with the cooked 'nduja to serve.

Xinjiang cumin goat skewers

MAKES ABOUT 12 SKEWERS

1 kg (2 lb 3 oz) deboned goat leg or shoulder,
  chopped into 1 cm (½ in) dice
5 tablespoons cumin seeds

MARINADE
180 ml (6 fl oz) light soy sauce
  (we use Healthy Boy brand)
180 ml (6 fl oz) soy bean paste
  (we use Healthy Boy brand)
180 ml (6 fl oz) Shaoxing rice wine
4 tablespoons Korean chilli powder
3 tablespoons five-spice
3 tablespoons sugar

In our experience travelling in China, the best way to eat these skewers is half-cut, standing outside on the street at 3 am after a good night out. But they're pretty good anywhere, any time. Lamb is a happy substitute if goat meat is unavailable.

Thread the goat onto 12 skewers, pushing the pieces together tightly. Heat a small frying pan over a medium heat and toast cumin seeds for 2–3 minutes, or until aromatic. Using a mortar and pestle, grind until coarse. Set aside.

Combine the marinade ingredients in a large bowl with three-quarters of the toasted ground cumin. Arrange the skewers snugly in a baking dish or container and pour over the marinade, turning skewers to coat well. Refrigerate for 6 hours, or overnight, to marinate, turning occasionally to coat well.

Remove skewers from fridge and bring to room temperature. Preheat your grill or barbecue to very high heat. Remove skewers from marinade, draining any excess, and cook for 2–3 minutes for medium-rare, turning constantly, until caramelised and charred.

Remove from the heat and sprinkle with the remaining toasted ground cumin. Serve immediately or, even better, eat with your hands standing around the barbecue, cold beer at hand.

Stuffed chicken wings

6 × chicken wings (approx. 80 g/7 oz) each),
  drumette removed

SEASONING MIX
½ teaspoon fennel seeds
1 star anise
6 white peppercorns
1 clove
½ cinnamon stick

FILLING
175 g (6¼ oz) minced (ground) chicken
3 shiitake mushrooms, finely diced
1 spring onion (scallion), finely chopped
1 garlic clove, finely chopped
40 ml (1¼ fl oz) soy sauce
25 ml (¾ fl oz) mirin

GLAZE
50 ml (1¾ fl oz) soy sauce
25 ml (¾ fl oz) maple syrup
10 ml (¼ fl oz) Tabasco Green Pepper Sauce

Chicken wings are versatile, easy to find and relatively cheap to buy. We believe those are attributes worth celebrating and we do that here by elevating the humble wing from bit player to star. As with any extreme makeover, it takes a little work. There are some simple butchering techniques involved in boning the chicken wing. But what might seem fiddly at first is actually pretty simple and a sure-fire way to impress your guests. And if a few wings get destroyed in the process, you can save those to make stock.

To make the seasoning mix

Cook spices in a frying pan over a medium heat, stirring frequently, for around 2–3 minutes or until lightly and evenly toasted (take care as they can burn quickly – you will know when they're ready as you'll smell the aromas). Transfer to a mortar and pestle and pound until finely ground. Set aside to cool.

To make the filling

Combine all the filling ingredients in a large bowl. Add the seasoning mix and mix well until all the ingredients are well combined.

Run the tip of the knife along the bone towards the wing tip, being careful not to pierce the skin. Keep tracing around the two bones in the wing until you have freed all the meat away from the bone as far down towards the tip as possible. Now, with your hands, hold onto the tip and pull the two bones away (you might need to bend it to dislocate the joint so it pulls away). Repeat with remaining wings.

Using the handle of a teaspoon, scoop small amounts of the filling mixture into each of the deboned wings, filling them up as much as you can but making sure to leave enough space to seal. To seal, thread a toothpick through the open end. Place the stuffed wings into the fridge for an hour to set or overnight.

To make the glaze, and cook

Preheat the oven to 180°C (360°F). Line a large roasting tray with baking paper. Whisk the glaze ingredients together in a small bowl. Place the stuffed wings in the tray, making sure they are not crowded.

Bake the wings for about 15 minutes or until they start to colour. Remove from the oven and baste with the glaze, then cook for a further 30 minutes, basting every 10 minutes or so. Remove from the oven and set aside to rest for 5 minutes before serving.

Bacon sandwich

MAKES 4 SANDWICHES

12 slices good-quality thick-cut
   double smoked bacon
A slab of cultured butter, at room temperature
8 slices crusty white bread, or 4 soft baps
8 tablespoons Gentleman's relish (see below)

GENTLEMAN'S RELISH

MAKES APPROX. 900 G (2 LB)

This recipe makes a good amount, more than you need for four sandwiches. Jar it, gift it to friends or store it in the fridge, for up to a month, and you'll soon find yourself reaching for it to accompany many other things. It is great served with a terrine or even a steak.

250 g (9 oz) pitted prunes
200 g (7 oz) tomato sauce (ketchup)
250 ml (8½ oz/1 cup) apple-cider vinegar
60 ml (2 fl oz) water
50 ml (1¾ fl oz) Worcestershire sauce
65 g (2¼ oz) brown sugar
80 g (2¾ oz) molasses
2 spring onions (scallions)
2 anchovy fillets
2 garlic cloves, chopped
pinch of ground cloves
pinch of mustard powder
pinch of ground allspice
2 pinches of ground black pepper
pinch of chilli powder

Place all ingredients in a heavy based stainless-steel pot over a medium heat. Bring to a gentle simmer and cook for 40 minutes, stirring from time to time.

When ready, set the pot aside to cool to room temperature. Once cooled, purée in a blender and pass through a fine sieve to achieve a smooth consistency.

The uncomplicated and unashamed simplicity of this sandwich is its strength. Resist the urge to add a fried egg, or anything else for that matter, because it won't make it any better. It's more desirable and indulgent without.

Cooking bacon is a personal thing. Some people like to cook it until it is crispy and almost burnt. Others like to cook it lightly, keeping it juicy and tender. We like it either way for this sandwich. Cook the bacon to your liking in a frying pan over a medium heat until golden and the fat has rendered somewhat. Transfer to paper towel to drain.

Meanwhile, butter the bread with an unhealthy amount of butter. Slather each slice of bread with 1 tablespoon of the gentleman's relish.

Stack the bacon evenly across 4 slices of bread and top with the last pieces of bread. Press gently to make the sandwiches 'stick'. Rest for a moment before cutting in half, then find a quiet corner to eat in private. It drips.

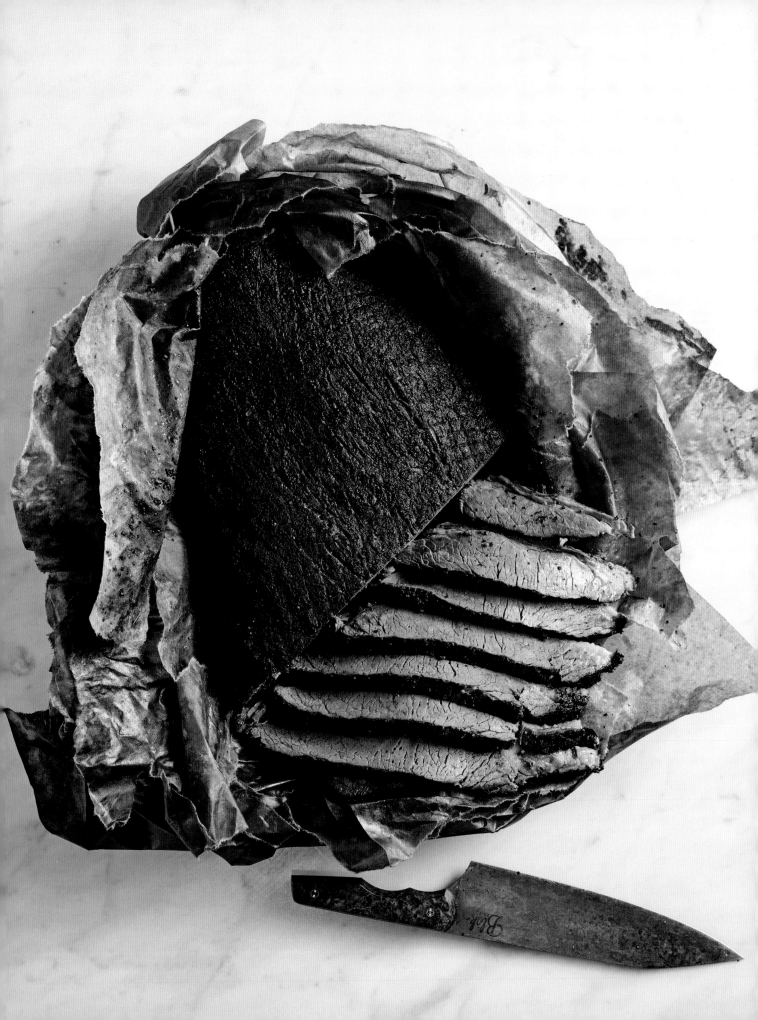

HOW TO MAKE BACKYARD PASTRAMI

This is a choose-your-own-adventure recipe. Whether you call it backyard pastrami or smoked brisket depends on if you rub the meat with the pastrami spices. Either version is delicious. This recipe involves time, forward planning and a charcoal barbecue, so the 'casual' in this equation is all about the eating, not the preparation. You can reduce some of the prep time by buying a pre-brined brisket from your butcher (remember to call ahead) rather than brining your own, which takes seven days.

Backyard pastrami

SERVES 8

1 × 4 kg (8 lb 13 oz) beef brisket

BASIC BRINE
8 litres (270 fl oz) water
25 g (1 oz) saltpetre (see Glossary, page 247)
440 g (15½ oz) salt
200 g (7 oz) brown sugar

PASTRAMI SPICE MIX
3 tablespoons cracked black pepper
1 tablespoon crushed coriander seeds
1 tablespoon ground coriander seeds
1 tablespoon brown sugar
1 tablespoon paprika
2 tablespoons garlic powder
2 tablespoons onion powder
1 teaspoon mustard seeds
1 teaspoon mustard powder

To make the brine

Combine the water, saltpetre, salt and sugar in a large non-reactive container, such as glass, plastic or stainless steel, and stir until sugar and salts have dissolved. Place in the fridge to cool to below 5°C (41°F).

Trim the brisket of excess fat, leaving about a 1 cm (½ in) layer. Place the brisket in the brine, making sure it is fully submerged. Cover the container and place in the fridge for 1 week, turning the brisket once a day. After 1 week, remove the brisket from the brine and pat dry with paper towel. Place in the fridge until ready to cook.

To make the pastrami spice mix

Combine all the ingredients in a bowl.

To cook the brisket

Remove the brisket from the fridge approximately 1 hour before you are ready to cook. Place on a large baking tray and rub all over with the pastrami spice mix.

Set aside to rest while you prepare the barbecue.

Light enough charcoal to fill your chimney starter. Once lit, pile the charcoal to one side. Place a small stainless-steel bowl full of water on the opposite side. Preheat the barbecue to around 90–95°C (190–200°F). Place the seasoned brisket on the opposite side to the charcoal and over the top of the bowl of water. Place a few little chunks of your favourite wood for smoking on top of the charcoal and close the lid.

Cook for 8 hours. It's a good idea to light another chimney full of charcoal about 4 hours into the cook, so you can use it to keep adding to the barbecue to keep the temperature consistent.

After 8 hours, wrap the brisket tightly in aluminium foil. Increase barbecue temperature to about 130–135°C (265–275°F). Return the brisket to the barbecue, close the lid and cook for a further 2–3 hours or until the internal temperature has reached 92°C (200°F).

Remove the brisket, wrap in a towel and store in an empty cooler box until you are ready to slice (it will remain hot for around 3 hours).

We serve our pastrami two ways

Pastrami sandwich

2 slices rye bread
butter, at room temperature
4 thick slices pastrami brisket, gently warmed
2 tablespoons Russian dressing (see recipe, right)
2 dill pickles, finely sliced lengthways

Spread each slice of bread generously with butter. Layer 1 slice of bread with sliced pastrami and top each pastrami slice with 2 spoonfuls of Russian dressing, pickles and the remaining slice of bread.

Pastrami plate

400 g (14 oz) finely shredded savoy cabbage
1 tablespoon dijon mustard
150 ml (5 fl oz) pickle juice from your pickle jar
salt and pepper, to season
1 tablespoon each dill and chives, chopped
1 thick slice pastrami brisket, gently warmed
1 tablespoon Gentleman's relish (page 59, optional)

Place cabbage in a large bowl. Whisk the mustard, pickle juice and a pinch of salt and pepper in a small bowl to combine. Pour mustard dressing over the shredded cabbage, add dill and chives and toss to combine. Place brisket slices on a plate alongside the cabbage mixture and a dollop of the gentleman's relish.

RUSSIAN DRESSING

MAKES 250 ML/ 8½ FL OZ/1 CUP

125 g (4½ oz/½ cup) mayonnaise (page 243)
125 g (4½ oz/½ cup) your favourite chilli sauce
1 teaspoon smoked hot paprika
1 tablespoon prepared (jarred) horseradish
1 teaspoon chopped tinned or jarred roasted peppers
1 teaspoon Worcestershire sauce
10 small chives, finely chopped

Place all the ingredients, except the finely chopped chives, in a blender and pulse until combined. Stir through the chives. Store the dressing in an airtight container in the fridge for up to 2 weeks.

SALADS &

VEGETABLES

Fig and jamon salad

SERVES 4

50 ml (1¾ fl oz /1 cup) rice vinegar
50 ml (1¾ fl oz /1 cup) water
1 tsp caster (superfine) sugar
12 blackberries
120 g (4½ oz) almonds
1 head of Castelfranco radicchio,
    leaves separated
8 figs
8 slices jamon Iberico

CRÈME FRAÎCHE AND MUSTARD DRESSING
6 tablespoons crème fraîche
½ teaspoon grated lemon zest
4 teaspoons lemon juice
4 teaspoons dijon mustard
salt and pepper, to season

This is a super simple, well-balanced salad that ticks all the flavour boxes. The crème fraîche and mustard dressing balances out the acidity from the pickled blackberries beautifully. Fig-wise, use whatever's in season and super ripe but, if you have a choice, lean towards sweeter, more jammy black figs rather than the drier-style green ones.

Combine the vinegar, water and sugar in a bowl and whisk until the sugar has dissolved. Add the blackberries, cover and set aside.

Make the dressing by whisking all the ingredients together in a large bowl. Season to taste and set aside.

Heat a frying pan over a medium heat, and toast the almonds for 3–4 minutes or until lightly golden. Remove from the heat, then roughly chop in half once cooled slightly.

To assemble the salad, wash and dry the radicchio and place in a bowl. Add the dressing and toss to combine. Arrange the leaves on a large serving dish. Tear the figs and jamon and arrange over the lettuce. Remove blackberries from the pickling juice and add to the salad, along with a little of the pickling juice. Sprinkle with almonds to serve.

Grilled quail and freekeh salad

SERVES 4

SALAD

2 tablespoons unsalted butter
2 celery stalks, finely chopped
2 golden shallots, finely chopped
1 clove garlic, finely chopped
200 g (7 oz) whole wheat freekeh
750 ml (25½ fl oz/3 cups) water
1 tablespoon barberries, soaked in water
  (see Glossary, page 247)
2 teaspoons finely chopped preserved
  lemon rind
3 tablespoons toasted almonds, chopped
2 tablespoons finely sliced spring onion
  (scallions)
10 g (¼ oz/¼ cup) each shredded mint
  and flat-leaf (Italian) parsley
3 teaspoons lemon juice
4 tablespoons extra-virgin olive oil
1 teaspoon chardonnay vinegar
salt and black pepper, to season

GRILLED QUAIL

4 jumbo (approximately 250 g/9 oz each)
  quail, butterflied
1 tablespoon pomegranate molasses
1 tablespoon hot water
1 teaspoon thyme leaves
2 tablespoons extra-virgin olive oil
¼ teaspoon coarse ground black pepper
½ teaspoon salt flakes

TO SERVE

juice of 1 lemon
60 g (2 oz/¼ cup) labneh or Greek-style yoghurt
harissa, optional

Quail is great and grilled quail is even better. And it's certainly great friends with this whole wheat salad.

To make the salad

Melt the butter in a stainless-steel saucepan with a tight-fitting lid over a low heat. Add the celery, shallot and garlic, and cook for about 5 minutes until the celery is soft.

Add the freekeh and stir to coat grains, then add water and bring to the boil. Cover with a lid, then reduce the heat to very low and cook for about 50–60 minutes, until the freekeh is tender and the water is fully absorbed (if the grains are cooked through and water is not fully absorbed, strain the grains and discard the excess liquid). Spread the cooked freekeh out on a tray to cool (it will keep in an airtight container in the fridge for up to 2 days).

Place the freekeh, barberries, preserved lemon, almonds, spring onion, mint and parsley in a large bowl and toss to combine. Combine the lemon juice, olive oil and vinegar and drizzle over the freekeh mixture, stirring to combine. Season to taste and arrange on a serving platter.

To grill the quail

Place the quail skin-side down on a baking tray. Combine the pomegranate molasses, water, thyme leaves, olive oil, black pepper and salt in a small bowl. Using a pastry brush, brush a generous amount of the mixture over the quail. Turn the birds over and brush the skin, coating evenly and using up all the mixture.

Place the quail in the fridge for an hour or so or until you are ready to cook. Prepare your fire or barbecue.

Cook the quail, skin-side down, over a medium heat for about 2 minutes, then turn and cook for a further 2–3 minutes. The skin will colour, blister and caramelise quickly so keep a close eye to ensure they don't burn. Place on barbecue rack, close the lid and cook for a final 4–6 minutes. Remove from the heat, and transfer to a plate to rest for at least 1–2 minutes. Squeeze over lemon juice and serve with the freekeh salad, labneh or yoghurt, and harissa, if heat is your thing.

Lentil salad with saltwater duck, watercress and pickled walnuts

SERVES 6

SALTWATER DUCK
4 tablespoons salt
2½ tablespoons white peppercorns
6 duck legs (approximately 240 g/8½ oz each)
2 star anise
3 cloves
2 teaspoons cumin seeds
3 bay leaves
1 cinnamon stick
2 teaspoons whole black peppercorns
5 slices fresh ginger
3 spring onions (scallions), cut into
   large segments

LENTILS
200 g (7 oz) Puy lentils
700 ml (23½ fl oz) chicken stock
salt and freshly ground black pepper, to season

MUSTARD DRESSING
1 tablespoon dijon mustard
½ tablespoon red wine vinegar
3 tablespoons extra-virgin olive oil
½ tablespoon pickled walnut juice (reserved
   from walnuts you use to serve)

TO SERVE
100 g (3½ oz) watercress
250 g (9 oz) jarred pickled walnuts
cracked pepper, to season

It is a process preparing the duck for this salad; however, once cooked, it is a cinch to bring together. The duck can easily be prepared a day or two in advance and benefits from this extra time in the poaching liquid. If sparklingly beautiful watercress is unavailable, the heart of frisée lettuce is a great substitute.

To make the saltwater duck

Toast the salt and white peppercorns in a frying pan over a medium heat, stirring frequently, for about 5–8 minutes until toasted. Remove from heat and set aside to cool.

Place the duck legs in a large bowl, cover with the toasted salt and white pepper mixture and massage the mixture into the duck. Cover and refrigerate for at least 3 hours to marinate.

Fill a 10–12 litre (approx. 3 gallon) stockpot or large saucepan three-quarters full with water. Add star anise, cloves, cumin, bay leaves, cinnamon, black peppercorns, ginger and spring onion and bring to the boil. Reduce heat to low, cover with a lid and simmer for 45 minutes. Remove from heat and reserve until the duck has been marinated.

Add duck legs and all of the marinating mixture to the pot, place over medium heat and bring to the boil. Once boiling, reduce to a very low simmer and cook for 1½ hours. Remove from heat, cover with lid and set aside to rest for 45 minutes.

Meanwhile, prepare the lentils. Place lentils and chicken stock in a large saucepan over a medium heat, bring to a gentle simmer and cook for approximately 30 minutes, or until tender. Remove from heat, season with salt and pepper and set aside to rest for 10 minutes.

To make the dressing
Whisk together the ingredients until well combined.

To serve, wash the watercress, remove any large stems, and arrange over the top of the dish. Spoon the lentils onto a serving plate. Remove the duck from the cooking liquid, pull apart into small chunks and arrange on the lentils (or serve one whole duck leg per person). Drizzle the mustard dressing over the salad. Dice up some of the pickled walnuts and arrange over the top. Finish with a good amount of fresh cracked pepper.

Roast partridge, farro and pickled black currant grapes

SERVES 4

2 whole partridges (approximately 900 g/
    2 lb each)
100 g (3½ oz/½ cup) farro
2 tablespoons unsalted butter
1 onion, finely diced
1 celery stalk, finely diced
1 tablespoon dried porcini, soaked in hot water
½ × 420 g (15 oz) tinned cooked peas, drained
2 tablespoons water
4 pickled vine leaves, soaked in hot water
2 tablespoons extra-virgin olive oil, plus extra
    for brushing
3 tablespoons Pickled black currant grapes
    (page 92)
1 teaspoon lemon juice
1 tablespoon flat-leaf (Italian) parsley,
    roughly chopped
1 tablespoon pistachios, roughly chopped
salt and freshly ground black pepper, to season

Partridge and pheasant are two seasonal game birds that are only available for short periods during winter. Partridges are smaller and have dark breast meat that's like a duck/quail combo in terms of flavour and texture. Pheasant is a larger bird with bolder, darker, gamier meat. Because partridge are hyper-seasonal, you need to get organised and order ahead of time, as they're not something many butchers hold as a matter of course (though that's not always the case in the UK). If it's not the right time of year, this recipe still works perfectly with one small chicken, four quails or a medium-sized pheasant.

Remove partridges from the fridge a few hours before you want to cook them.

Place farro in a small saucepan, cover with water, place over medium heat and bring to a simmer. Cook for 40 minutes or until tender.

Gently warm 1 tablespoon of the butter in a small frying pan. Add onion and cook for around 5 minutes until tender. Add the celery and cook for a further 2 minutes until soft. Remove the porcini from the soaking water, discarding the water. Chop the porcini, add to the onion mixture and cook for a few moments. Add the cooked farro to the onion mixture, and add the peas and water. Continue to cook for a few minutes until the liquid has been absorbed. Cover and set aside to rest.

Meanwhile, preheat the oven to 180°C (360°F). Rinse the vine leaves under cold water and pat dry with paper towel. Lay on a baking tray and brush both sides of the vine leaves with olive oil. Bake for 3–5 minutes until the leaves dry, buckle and become crispy.

Increase the oven temperature to 190°C (375°F). Brush the partridges with 1 tablespoon of the olive oil and season with salt. Heat the remaining olive oil with the remaining tablespoon of butter in a large, ovenproof frying pan over medium heat. Add the partridges and cook for 5 minutes, turning in the pan to brown all over.

Now sit the partridges upright and transfer the pan to the oven and roast for 10 minutes. Remove pan from the oven and separate the legs from the crown (the breasts on the bone). Set the crown aside to rest and place the legs on a baking tray. Return to the oven for a further 10 minutes.

Meanwhile, assemble the salad. Toss the farro with 2 tablespoons of the pickled grapes, lemon juice, parsley and pistachios. Season to taste with salt and pepper.

Remove the legs from the oven and set aside, together with the crown, for a further 10 minutes. Remove the breast fillets. Spoon around 3 tablespoons of the farro salad onto each plate and top each with a leg and a fillet. Top with the crisp vine leaves and sprinkle each plate with 1 teaspoon of the pickled grapes. If you are using quail, serve the bird whole on the plate alongside the salad and vine leaves.

Fennel, celery heart and pecorino salad

SERVES 4

1 tablespoon dijon mustard
50 ml (1¾ fl oz) lemon juice
1 teaspoon honey
pinch of salt
100 ml (3½ fl oz) extra-virgin olive oil
1 bunch celery
2 fennel bulbs
135 g (5 oz) hard pecorino, shaved
freshly ground black pepper, to season

You're only using the young, tender and sweet heart of the celery for this salad, but keep all the tougher outer celery stalks to make stock (see Staple recipes, page 242) or soup. This salad goes brilliantly with rare-grilled lamb backstraps.

Combine the mustard, lemon juice, honey and salt in a small bowl. Slowly pour in the olive oil, whisking the ingredients together. Set aside while you prepare the fennel and celery.

Remove the large outer stalks of celery and store in the fridge for another use. Remove the top woody part of the fennel and discard any damaged outer layers. Cut the celery heart and fennel bulbs into thin slices, about ½ cm (approx. ¼ in) thick (a mandoline is useful for this). Keep some of the tender celery leaves to garnish the salad.

Place celery and fennel in a large bowl and drizzle with the dressing. Gently fold through the dressing. Arrange on a serving platter. Top with shaved pecorino and plenty of black pepper.

Bread salad

SERVES 4

SOURDOUGH CROUTONS
1 × 5 cm (2 in) thick slice sourdough bread
2 tablespoons extra-virgin olive oil
pinch of salt

SALAD
3 large tomatoes, sliced
½ Lebanese cucumber, peeled and diced
4 red radishes, sliced
4 spring onions (scallions), finely chopped
3 mild long green chillies, seeded and
    finely chopped
10 sprigs flat-leaf (Italian) parsley,
    finely chopped
10 green olives, pitted and roughly chopped

DRESSING
80 ml (2½ fl oz/⅓ cup) extra-virgin olive oil
juice of ½ lemon
1 garlic clove, chopped
1 tablespoon white wine vinegar
pinch of salt
black pepper

Bread salad is a dish we prepare throughout the year. It changes with the seasons so no two we've thrown together have ever been the same. This summer version is the current favourite.

To make the croutons, preheat the oven to 180°C (360°F). Cut the crust off the bread and tear into 2 cm (¾ in) chunks. Place in a bowl and drizzle with oil, tossing to coat the pieces evenly. Season with salt, transfer to a baking tray and roast for about 10–15 minutes or until golden. Set aside.

Combine all the salad ingredients in a large bowl. Whisk the dressing ingredients together and pour over the salad. We like to leave this salad for a few hours at room temperature to marinate. Just before serving, season to taste. Add the croutons and stir well – the bread will happily soak up all the lovely juices. Serve immediately.

Charred sugarloaf cabbage with kombu butter

SERVES 4

2 × 2.5 cm (1 in) pieces dried kombu
   (see Glossary, page 247)
120 ml (4 fl oz) grapeseed oil
1 large sugarloaf (hispi/pointed) cabbage,
   outer leaves removed, halved
150 g (5½ oz) unsalted butter
300 ml (10 fl oz) chicken stock
1 tablespoon apple-cider vinegar
salt, to season
8 slices lardo (optional)

This dish lends itself to a really cold winter night. It's an amazing dish on its own but it also sits well alongside slow-cooked lamb shoulder or game. Cooking the sugarloaf (hispi/pointed) cabbage with kombu and butter adds a rich umami element to the sweet, charred cabbage and finishing it with buttery lardo adds another layer of richness. The pointed sugarloaf is excellent for this dish: it's structurally resilient under high heat and its compressed leaves are perfect for soaking up all the butter and kombu flavours. If you can't find it, use half of a very firm Savoy cabbage.

Preheat oven to 180°C (360°F).

Using tongs, hold the kombu over an open flame for about 2 minutes, turning often, until lightly toasted. Set aside to cool. Transfer to a spice mill or use a mortar and pestle to grind into a fine powder.

Heat the oil in an ovenproof skillet over a medium-high heat. Cook the cabbage, cut-side down, undisturbed for 10–15 minutes, until the underside is blackened (the edge of the sides will start to brown as well).

Reduce heat to medium-low, add all but two knobs of the butter to the skillet and shake the pan to help the butter get around and under the cabbage. As soon as the butter is melted and foaming, tilt the skillet towards you and spoon the browning butter over the cabbage, being sure to bathe the area around the thickest part. Add the chicken stock and vinegar and place the skillet in the oven for 20 minutes – or until the cabbage is tender. Remove from the oven, add the remaining butter and the toasted kombu powder, return to medium-heat on the stovetop and baste with the butter and kombu for a further 5 minutes.

Transfer the cabbage to a cutting board and cut into 2 halves. Reserve the cooking juices in the pan. Pull leaves open slightly and season with salt.

Arrange the lardo over the warm cabbage and leave to sit for 1–2 minutes for the lardo to soften. Transfer to a serving plate and dress with the reserved juices from the pan.

Jansson's temptation

SERVES 8

1 tablespoon softened butter
6 medium desiree potatoes, rinsed and cut into
   large matchsticks (do use a mandoline)
80 g (2¾ oz) anchovy fillets
5 large golden shallots, diced
500 ml (17 fl oz/2 cups) pouring
   (whipping) cream
½ teaspoon salt flakes
pinch of white pepper
extra 50 g (1¾ oz) cold unsalted butter, diced

This Swedish Christmas favourite was named (according to some) after a food-loving Swedish opera singer called Pelle Janzon, who was singing his heart out in the early 1900s. Andrew first learned to cook this dish from chef Walter Bourke, a former ballet dancer and influential Melbourne chef, whose wife Maria is Swedish. It's layered with anchovies, smothered in cream and baked, so you can't go wrong. Don't wait for Christmas.

Preheat the oven to 190°C (375°F). If you are using a fan-forced oven, turn off the fan, we find conventional heat is better for this recipe.

Butter the base of a 20 × 26 cm (8 × 10 in) ceramic baking dish (or a round ovenproof dish of a similar size) with the soft butter. Layer 1 cm (½ in) of the potatoes in the base of the dish. Evenly arrange one-third of the anchovies and one-third of the shallot over the potato. Repeat twice more with remaining anchovies, shallot and potato, finishing with a layer of potato.

Combine cream, salt and pepper in a small saucepan over a medium heat and bring to a simmer. Immediately pour over the potatoes. Top with the diced butter. Bake for 1 hour or until the potatoes are soft when pierced with a knife (if they seem a little firm, cook for a further 10 minutes or until cooked). Set aside for 30 minutes to rest or until ready to serve. Return to the oven for 15 minutes to reheat when you wish to serve.

Asparagus with sauce bâtarde and dried olives

SERVES 4

2 tablespoons extra-virgin olive oil
16 spears asparagus, trimmed
juice of ½ lemon
salt, to season

SAUCE
2 tablespoons thick (double/heavy) cream
3 egg yolks
pinch of salt
175 g (6 oz) unsalted butter
175 g (6 oz) plain (all-purpose) flour
225 ml hot water, boiled and left for 5 minutes
  to cool
zest and juice of ½ lemon

DRIED OLIVES
250 ml (8½ fl oz/1 cup) water
220 g (8 oz/1 cup) white sugar
250 g (9 oz) your favourite black olives, drained,
  rinsed and pitted

Sauce bâtarde is kind of a 'cheat's' hollandaise – butter-based and quite stable so you can make it in advance and then bring it back to heat without it splitting (something the more sensitive and dramatic hollandaise won't allow you to do). The salty, crisp, dried olive element here is non-negotiable. You could use the dried olive to season a roast chicken (page 125), or even to season a resting steak (page 141). Try sauce bâtarde on poached eggs, grilled beans or roast pork.

To make the sauce

Whisk together the cream and egg yolks with a pinch of salt. Add butter to a saucepan over a medium heat. Once melted, whisk in the flour, then the hot water. Remove from the heat and slowly whisk in the egg and cream mixture, followed by the lemon zest and juice, and whisk briefly to combine. Leave the sauce in a warm spot until ready to use.

To make the olives

Preheat the oven to 100°C (215°F). Place the water and sugar in a saucepan over a medium heat and bring to a simmer until sugar has dissolved. In two batches, add olives and cook for about 2 minutes until blanched, removing with a slotted spoon. Discard the cooking syrup.

Increase the oven temperature to 120°C (250°F). Place the blanched olives on a baking tray lined with baking paper, and place in the oven for about 4 hours or until olives are dry. If after 4 hours they still feel a little wet, keep cooking them for another 45 minutes to an hour. Once they are dried, they will keep in an airtight container for up to 1 month.

To cook the asparagus and serve

Heat olive oil in a large frying pan over a high heat and cook the asparagus, turning every 10 seconds, until it is charred around the outside. Remove from the heat and season with lemon juice. Gently warm the sauce in a small saucepan. In a mortar and pestle, crush the dried olives to a rough crumb.

Arrange the asparagus on a serving plate, spoon over the sauce and finish with a spoonful of the crushed dried olive sprinkled over the top.

Carrots with smoked yoghurt

SERVES 6

200 g (7 oz) plain yoghurt
handful of wood chips, for smoking
1 tablespoon honey
3 tablespoons extra-virgin olive oil
1 long red chilli, seeded and finely chopped
1 tablespoon oregano leaves
zest and juice of 1 lemon
1 tablespoon unsalted butter, melted
2 bunches Dutch carrots
5 thyme sprigs
salt and freshly ground black pepper, to season

To peel or not to peel, this is the question that has still not been resolved in our kitchen. For this preparation, however, we like to use the finest Dutch carrots we can find, where the skin is thin and brings so much flavour to the dish. If using larger conventional carrots or heirloom carrots, do peel them, as the skin can get bitter and prevents any outside flavours from penetrating the flesh.

To make the smoked yoghurt and dressing

Spread the yoghurt out on a small tray and keep it cold in the fridge. Tear off a sheet of aluminium foil about the size of an A4 sheet of paper. Fold it in half twice into a smaller square, and turn up the sides so it resembles a small tray. Pinch the corners so it stays together.

Place the aluminium tray at one end of a large roasting tray and fill it with wood chips. Tear off 2 more larger sheets of aluminium foil big enough to cover your roasting tray. Remove the small tray of yoghurt from the fridge and keep it close to your larger tray.

Using a blowtorch, light the wood chips. Once they are lit, blow out the flames and quickly place the small tray with the yoghurt at the opposite end to the smouldering wood chips. Cover the whole roasting tray with the larger pieces of aluminium foil that you prepared, making sure it is tight and trapping in all the smoke.

Leave it covered for approximately 20 minutes. Uncover and remove the smaller tray of yoghurt. Give it a mix with a spoon and transfer it to an airtight container. It will keep refrigerated for up to 1 week.

To make the dressing, whisk the honey, 2 tablespoons of the olive oil and a pinch of salt together in a medium sized bowl. Add the chilli, oregano, lemon zest and juice. Set aside until ready to serve.

To cook the carrots and assemble the salad

Bring a large saucepan of salted water to the boil. Cook the carrots until tender, depending on the size it will take anything from 3–10 minutes (use a small paring knife to check if the carrots are tender, there needs to be a slight resistance). Once ready, remove the carrots from the water and drain.

Heat a large heavy based fry pan over medium heat, if the carrots don't fit in the pan, cook the carrots in two batches. Add the butter and the remaining tablespoon of olive oil followed by the carrots and sauté, shuffling around in the pan until golden, caramelised and tender, around 3–6 minutes. Add the thyme sprigs for the last minute of cooking and toss the carrots and thyme together in the pan. Season to taste.

Place the carrots in a bowl with the dressing. Taste and season with a pinch of salt and leave the carrots to marinate at room temperature for half an hour or so. To serve, arrange the smoked yoghurt on a serving platter, and top with the marinated carrots.

Tomato salad with shallot dressing

SERVES 4

3 large golden shallots, finely diced
2 large heirloom tomatoes, sliced in ½ cm (¼ in)
   slices or halved horizontally
1 tablespoon aged Sherry vinegar
3 tablespoons extra-virgin olive oil
sea salt, to season

The simplicity of this dish underlines the imperative to only make this salad (and anything else with fresh tomatoes in it) with the best tomatoes you can get your hands on.

Place the shallot in a small bowl and season with a little salt. Arrange the tomato slices on a platter in a single layer (or place the halves, if using, onto single serving plates) and season with a pinch of salt. Top each slice (or half) of tomato with a generous amount of the diced shallot. Mix the vinegar and olive oil together and spoon over the tomatoes.

Broccolini with nettle pesto

SERVES 4

NETTLE PESTO
250 g (9 oz) nettles (about half a bunch, to yield
   ½ cup blanched)
2 garlic cloves
40 g (1½ oz/¼ cup) toasted pine nuts
25 g (1 oz/¼ cup) grated Grana Padano
40 ml (1¼ fl oz) olive oil
salt, to season

PICKLED BLACK CURRANT GRAPES
½ teaspoon whole allspice
6 cloves
½ teaspoon coriander seeds
6 thin slices fresh ginger
½ teaspoon mustard seeds
300 ml (10 fl oz) white vinegar
100 ml (3½ fl oz) water
150 g (5½ oz) caster (superfine) sugar
200 g (7 oz) black currant grapes

GRILLED BROCCOLINI
1 tablespoon olive oil
2 bunches broccolini (tenderstem broccoli),
   about 400 g/14 oz
salt, to season
juice of ½ lemon

For this combination of charred broccolini and pickled black currant grapes, it's a case of the fresher the better, so aim to make it just before serving.

To make the nettle pesto

To protect your hands against the nettles' sting, use gloves when handling the raw nettles. Remove the leaves and discard the stems. Bring a saucepan of salted water to the boil over a high heat. Cook the nettles for 1 minute. Remove from the heat and strain the nettles in a colander. Quickly drop the nettles into a bowl of iced water for 2 minutes. Strain through the colander again and dry the nettles in clean kitchen towel, making sure you have removed all the moisture. Now that they have been blanched, they can be handled freely.

Place the blanched nettles, garlic, pine nuts and a pinch of salt in a food processor. Pulse a few times until the mixture starts to come together, then add the Grana Padano and olive oil and pulse a few more times to combine. You don't want to overwork the pesto, so short bursts will keep it from blending too fine. We suggest keeping it quite chunky. Add more oil if it needs to be loosened up a bit. Taste and adjust with salt to your liking.

To make the pickled grapes

Place all the ingredients except the grapes in a large saucepan. Bring to a simmer and immediately remove from the heat and leave to cool. Strain the pickling liquid and pour enough of the pickling liquid over the grapes to cover. This will make more than you need for this recipe.

To cook the broccolini

Heat the olive oil in a frying pan over medium heat. Cook the broccolini for about 4 minutes, turning frequently to cook evenly on all sides. Remove from the heat, season with salt and lemon juice. Arrange the broccolini on a serving plate, spoon the nettle pesto over the top, then arrange the pickled grapes over the dish (cut a few in half and leave a few whole).

Smoked pumpkin with chermoula

SERVES 4

CHERMOULA

1 teaspoon cumin seeds

1 teaspoon coriander seeds

45 g (1½ oz/1½ cups) coriander (cilantro), roughly chopped

15 g (½ oz/¾ cup) flat-leaf (Italian) parsley, roughly chopped

1 teaspoon roughly chopped fresh ginger

1 teaspoon thyme leaves

3 garlic cloves

200 ml (7 fl oz) extra-virgin olive oil

zest and juice of ½ lemon

½ teaspoon Aleppo chilli flakes (see Glossary, page 247)

½ teaspoon salt

SMOKED PUMPKIN

1 golden nugget pumpkin (approx. 1 kg/2 lb 2 oz)

a few handfuls of your favourite smoking wood (oak is a nice subtle flavour)

This will take 3–4 hours to cook but is surprisingly simple to prepare. Place the whole pumpkin into the barbecue, where it will slowly smoke and cook at the same time. Once cooked, break the charred exterior open to reveal the incredibly soft, sweet and smoky interior. Small golden nugget pumpkins are the best for this.

To make the chermoula

Toast the cumin and coriander seeds in a frying pan over a medium heat, stirring frequently, for 1–2 minutes until fragrant. Transfer to a mortar and pestle and crush the toasted seeds into a rough grind – it's ok if there are a few chunky bits. Place all of the remaining ingredients in a blender, add the ground spice and pulse until it all comes together as a chunky paste. Transfer to an airtight container.

To smoke the pumpkin

For best results, use a wood-fired grill or smoker. Light enough charcoal for a 3-hour cook (two chimneys full of charcoal). Once your charcoal is hot, place the coals to one side and adjust the grill or smoker to hold the temperature at 160°C (250°F). Place your whole pumpkin on the opposite side to the coals. Place a few small chunks of smoking wood on the coals and close the lid. Let the pumpkin cook undisturbed for 3 hours.

As the pumpkin cooks, regularly assess the progress by inserting a wooden skewer through the skin to feel if the pumpkin is tender and cooked.

To serve, cut the pumpkin in half. Using a large spoon, scoop out the seeds and discard. Slice the pumpkin into wedges and arrange on a serving plate, then top with chermoula.

Salsify with maple butter

SERVES 4

500 g (1 lb 2 oz) salsify (see Glossary, page 247)
juice of ½ lemon
500 ml (17 fl oz/2 cups) milk
1 bay leaf
10 peppercorns
2 sprigs thyme
a few flat-leaf (Italian) parsley stalks
2 tablespoons butter
1 tablespoon maple syrup
pinch of salt

When salsify is unavailable, you can replace this very seasonal root vegetable with parsnip for equally marvellous results. The caramelised nuttiness of this dish is one of our favourite things to eat with roast chicken (page 125).

Peel the salsify, placing it in a bowl of water with the lemon juice to prevent it from going brown. Slice the salsify into 6 cm (2½ in) lengths and place in a non-reactive saucepan. Pour over the milk and top up with water until salsify is immersed.

Add the bay leaf, peppercorns, thyme and parsley to the pan. Bring to a simmer, then reduce the heat and cook for about 10 minutes until the salsify is just tender but not too soft. Set aside in the milk mixture to cool to room temperature. Once cooled and you are ready to serve, strain.

Warm the butter and maple syrup in a large frying pan until bubbling. Add the salsify and a large pinch of salt. Cook for about 4–5 minutes, gently shaking the pan and turning the salsify from time to time with a spoon, until golden. Transfer to a serving plate and serve immediately.

MEZCAL MARGARITA – MEZCAL MULE – MEZCAL AND TONIC

FLATBREAD AND SCHMALTZ

GRILLED PADRÓN PEPPERS WITH BOTTARGA

VEAL LIVER SHEFTALIA

LUGANICA SAUSAGES, ROASTED PEPPER SAUCE

ASADO BEEF RIBS WITH SALSA ROJA

COS LETTUCE WITH RANCH DRESSING AND MINT

POTATOES COOKED IN COAL

A BUTCHER'S PICNIC

I love eating outdoors with family and friends. An ideal situation for me is sitting by water, whether that's by the ocean or beside a river in the bush, with a makeshift barbecue, cooking delicious food while everyone stands around having a few drinks, telling a few stories and reminiscing, with everyone also contributing their two cents' worth about how you should be cooking something on the grill.

The dishes I choose for a Butcher's Picnic are ones that can all be cooked on the same apparatus, a makeshift grill. I love making a rustic sauce by roasting off some vegetables and tomatoes with some good olive oil and seasoning – it goes brilliantly with grilled meats. To make your life easier, make your condiments ahead of time and take them with you. You can also pre-batch the cocktails then shake them with the ice from the Esky that's keeping the beers cold. There's something fancy about a properly chilled margarita in a rustic location.

Make sure you have a sturdy grill and some cinderblocks to build a windbreak for your grill. You should also invest in some long tongs or grill forks, and take along a few mixing bowls and serving plates, plus a nice big chopping board to do some preparation.

This picnic is about sharing, using your hands and eating off sharing plates. Keep it as simple as possible and just enjoy the moment.

TROY

HOW TO COOK WITH FIRE

Whether you have a kettle barbecue, or another type of wood-fired barbecue, the method of building your fire will depend on whether you want to use hot embers created from burning wood or heat good-quality lump charcoal for cooking. Either are totally fine.

To use lump charcoal, you will need a fire chimney (these are readily available from most hardware and barbecue stores). They are simple to use and quick to light. Most of the time you only need to fill one chimney's worth of coals to cook with, so it also helps with lighting the right amount, as most brands of chimneys are the same size. You simply fill the chimney with coals and place a fire lighter underneath. You will have hot coals in 15–20 minutes.

The best charcoal is Japanese binchotan, as it is extremely dense and will last up to four times longer than the more commonly seen ogatan. Due to its heat it also creates terrific caramelisation and flavour, different to any other cooking method.

To create coals from fire, you will require a bit more time and a dedicated space to burn off the wood. If you have both, the difference in the flavour imparted to your product from cooking with fresh coals is the best.

Building and burning down a fire for coals to cook with takes time, and quite a bit of wood to ensure you have enough coals to keep your heat consistent. Everyone has their own method on how to build and light a fire, but the most important thing to consider is airflow. You need enough draught air to keep the fire burning fast enough to create coals for cooking.

THE TYPES OF WOOD WE LIKE TO USE ARE:

MALLEE ROOT, which is a knotted section of a native eucalyptus tree. The wood is very hard and compact, which burns very hot and creates longer-lasting coals.

SPOTTED GUM, an Australian native mostly found on the east coast, is another hard wood that burns longer.

FRUIT TREE CUTTINGS are great for smoking. Trees like apple, cherry and grape vines all create a nice subtle smoke flavour.

Mezcal cocktails

Mezcal is a spirit made from agave that's produced in specific regions of Mexico. It has a fruity, earthy and smoky flavour. Traditionally it's drunk straight with some lime, salt and a little chilli; however, we've used it to reimagine some classic tequila-based cocktails – its smoky profile is the perfect accompaniment to meats cooked over the wood grill.

MEZCAL MARGARITA

SERVES 2

60 ml (1 fl oz) mezcal
60 ml (1 fl oz) tequila blanco
40 ml (1¼ fl oz) lime juice
30 ml (1 fl oz) Cointreau orange liqueur
2 wedges of lime
2 pinches of salt

Pour the mezcal, tequila, lime juice and Cointreau over ice in a cocktail shaker. Shake for a few minutes. Fill 2 medium glasses with ice and strain the shaken margarita into the glasses. Garnish with a wedge of lime and a pinch of salt.

MEZCAL MULE

SERVES 4

240 ml (8 fl oz) mezcal
60 ml (2 fl oz) lime juice
crushed ice
600 ml (20½ fl oz) ginger beer, to top up
6 wedges of lime

Pour the mezcal and lime juice into a 1 litre (approx. 1 quart) jug, give it a little stir and add crushed ice so the jug is half full. Top up with ginger beer. Fill 4 glasses with crushed ice. Pour the drink into the glasses and garnish with lime wedges.

MEZCAL AND TONIC

SERVES 4

120 ml (4 fl oz) mezcal
120 ml (4 fl oz) americano bianco vermouth
ice cubes
120 ml (4 fl oz) tonic water
4 grapefruit wedges

Pour the mezcal and vermouth into a tall jug. Half-fill the jug with ice, add the tonic and stir for a few seconds. Pour into glasses and finish each with a wedge of grapefruit.

Flatbread and schmaltz

SERVES 4

12.5 g (½ oz) dried yeast
250 ml (8½ fl oz/1 cup) water
2 teaspoons honey
3 tablespoons sheep's milk yoghurt
500 g (1 lb 2 oz) baker's flour, plus extra
   for dusting
10 g (¼ oz) sea salt
100 g (3½ oz) Schmaltz (see below)
salt and Espelette pepper (see Glossary,
   page 247), to season

SCHMALTZ

MAKES 200 G (7 OZ)

800 g (1 lb 12 oz) raw chicken skin and/or fat
1 onion, sliced

Put the chicken skin in a large heavy-based saucepan over a low heat and fill with enough water to just cover the skin. Bring to a slow simmer and cook for around 1 hour, or until the water has evaporated. Add the onion and cook until caramelised. Remove from the heat and strain the liquid into an airtight container. It will keep in the fridge for up to 1 month.

The rendered chicken fat steeped with cooked onions is called gribenes. They're delicious eaten with flatbread and a dollop of crème fraîche.

Moreish fluffy flatbread – the perfect vessel to carry your barbecue treats and to mop up the delicious juices left on your plate. Instead of butter or oil, we serve ours with schmaltz, a traditional Jewish and eastern European condiment made from rendered chicken or goose fat.

Combine yeast and water in the bowl of a stand mixer and leave for 5 minutes to activate the yeast. Add the honey and yoghurt and mix again for another 2 minutes. Add the flour and salt and, using the dough hook attachment, mix on medium speed for 10 minutes. Cover the mixing bowl with a damp tea (dish) towel and set aside in a warm place for around 1–2 hours until the dough roughly doubles in size.

Knock back the dough by kneading it a few times and roll into 8 small balls. Put on an oiled baking tray and cover with the tea (dish) towel then set aside to rest in a warm place for a further 45 minutes.

On a floured bench, using a rolling pin, roll out each ball to a circle approximately 5 mm (¼ in) thick. Leave the dough to rest for an hour before cooking. Put the rolled dough in the fridge if you plan on serving any later than this.

Brush both sides of each round with schmaltz. Grill, in batches, on a barbecue, or in a frying pan, over a medium heat for about 2–3 minutes on each side until golden brown. Brush again with schmaltz and season with salt and Espelette pepper to serve.

Grilled padrón peppers with bottarga

SERVES 4

Hailing from the northwest of Spain, but successfully grown in Victoria, these peppers are known as the Russian roulette of chillies. Most of them have a vibrant aromatic flavour, but one in ten are hot, which adds some excitement to the dish.

360 g (12½ oz) padrón peppers
2 tablespoons extra-virgin olive oil
salt, to season
juice of ½ lemon
10 g (¼ oz) bottarga

These can be cooked in a frying pan or on the barbecue. We also like to cook them on a wood-fired grill.

Preheat the grill to hot (or place a heavy-based frying pan over high heat). Combine peppers and olive oil in a large bowl. Grill the peppers until they are caramelised, moving them around frequently.

Once they are cooked, return them to the bowl you dressed them in and season with salt and lemon juice. Arrange on a plate and, using a fine grater or microplane, grate bottarga over the top. Enjoy while hot.

Veal liver sheftalia

SERVES 4

Sheftalia is a traditional Cypriot sausage usually made with lamb and pork mince, onion, parsley and black pepper. This is our version using veal liver, which is delicious cooked over a wood-fired grill.

1 kg (2 lb 3 oz) veal liver
700 ml (23½ fl oz) milk
4 sprigs rosemary, roughly chopped
½ bunch flat-leaf (Italian) parsley, roughly chopped
2 garlic cloves, smashed
1 red onion, roughly diced
pinch of salt
1 tablespoon olive oil
1 kg (2.2 lb) caul fat (see Glossary, page 247)
squeeze of lemon

Place the veal liver in a container and pour over the milk, making sure the liver is submerged. Cover and store in the fridge to marinate overnight. Strain, discarding milk, and pat the liver dry with paper towel. Cut the liver into slices about as thick as your finger. Put on a baking tray and return to the fridge while you prepare the other ingredients.

Pulse the rosemary, parsley, garlic and onion in a food processor a few times to combine. Add salt and olive oil, then pulse a few more times until you reach a slightly chunky consistency.

Spoon the marinade over the sliced liver, making sure it is fully coated. Set aside in the fridge to marinate for at least 1 hour.

Lay out the caul fat. Starting in a corner of the caul fat, place a slice of the marinated liver on top (ensuring the chunky marinade comes with it). Fold over the caul fat, wrap it twice, cut it away from the larger section of caul fat and tuck in the edges. Arrange in a dish. Repeat with remaining liver. These are best cooked on a barbecue, or over coals on a wood grill. They will cook quickly.

Prepare a wood grill or preheat the barbecue to high. Grill for 2 minutes then turn and cook for a further 2 minutes. Set aside to rest for a few minutes and serve with a squeeze of fresh lemon.

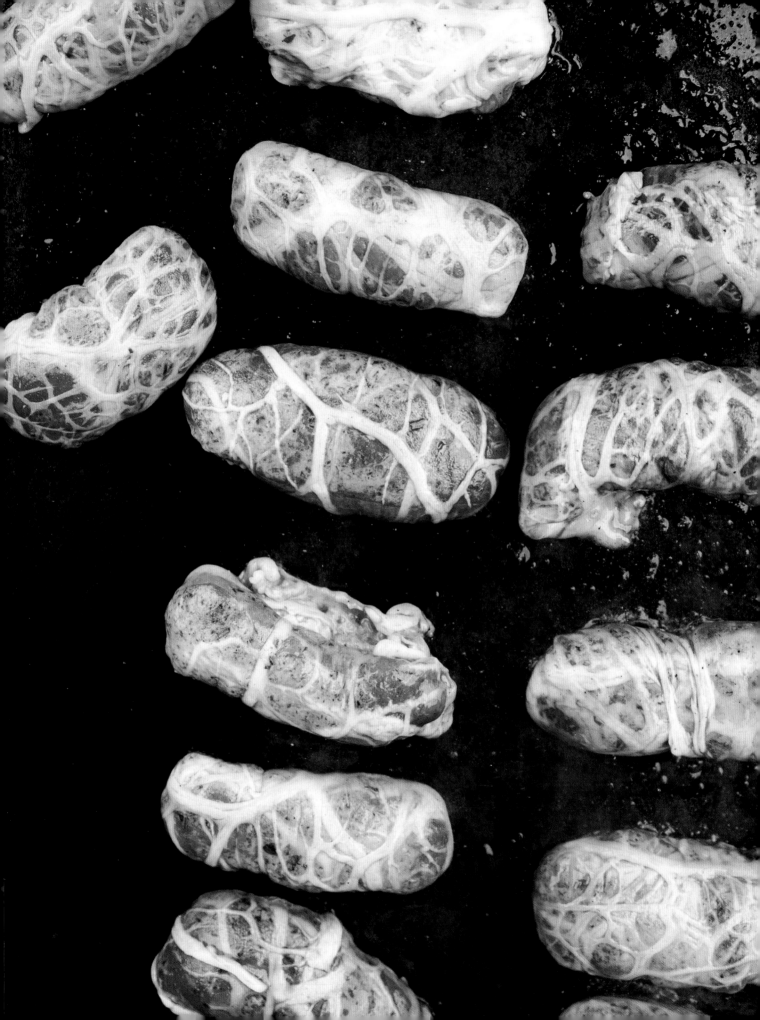

Luganica sausages, roasted pepper sauce

SERVES 6

SAUSAGES

1.8 kg (4 lb) coarsely minced (ground) pork
200 g (7 oz) coarsely minced (ground)
  pork back fat
30 g (1 oz) salt
10 g (¼ oz) fennel seeds, toasted
2 garlic cloves, finely minced
5 g (⅛ oz) Aleppo pepper (see Glossary,
  page 247)
30 g (1 oz) smoked paprika
200 ml (7 fl oz) white wine
1 × 23 mm length mutton casing (ask your
  butcher for fresh thin sausage casings)

ROASTED PEPPER SAUCE

4 banana peppers (see Glossary, page 247)
2 red capsicum (bell pepper)
2 × Tropea onions, skin on (see Glossary,
  page 247)
1 leek
2 roma tomatoes
4 garlic cloves
pinch of salt
6 anchovy fillets
2 tablespoons olive oil
1 teaspoon Sherry vinegar
salt, to season
½ bunch chives, finely chopped, to serve

Hailing from the north of Italy, luganica is a pork sausage rolled into a coil and cooked whole – making it an impressive centrepiece and great for sharing.

To make the sausages

Using a stand mixer fitted with the dough hook attachment, mix the pork, back fat and salt on medium speed for about 4 minutes. Add the fennel seeds, garlic, Aleppo pepper and paprika and mix for a further 4 minutes. Slowly add the white wine and mix for another 2 minutes.

Remove the mixing bowl from the stand and, using your hands, work the mix for another minute, making sure all the ingredients are combined and the mixture is tacky.

If you don't have a small sausage stuffer, use a small attachment for your stand mixer. Stuff the sausage casings on a low speed, making sure there are no air pockets. Portion each length into 300 g (10½ oz) and roll into a coil, fixing into place using bamboo skewers in a cross formation. The mixture should make 6–7 lengths of sausage, each about 20–24 cm (approx. 8–9½ in) long.

Prepare your fire or preheat the barbecue to high (light your barbecue with enough charcoal to last a few hours).

To make the roasted pepper sauce

Grill the peppers, capsicum, onions (skin on), leek and tomatoes over a hot grill for about 10 minutes, turning occasionally or until very well charred all over. Transfer to a large bowl, cover with aluminium foil and set aside for about 20 minutes to allow the vegetables to steam in their own heat.

Meanwhile, prepare the rest of the sauce. In a mortar and pestle, grind the garlic, salt and anchovies together to make a paste. Remove the foil from the bowl and peel away all the charred skin from the vegetables. Remove the seeds from the peppers and tomatoes, then roughly chop the flesh of all the charred ingredients.

Transfer to a food processor and add the garlic mixture. Add the olive oil and pulse a few times to bring all the ingredients together. You don't want to overwork it, it still needs to be a bit chunky.

Preheat a large frying pan on the barbecue to hot. Transfer the pepper mixture to the pan and cook for about 6–8 minutes, stirring frequently, until most of the moisture has evaporated from the pan. Season with Sherry vinegar and salt. Remove from the grill and set aside to rest.

Meanwhile, grill the sausages over direct heat for about 4–5 minutes then turn and cook for a further 4–5 minutes. If the grill is really hot, you might want to turn them more frequently so they don't burn.

To serve, remove the skewers, and arrange sausages on a serving plate. Spoon over the sauce, sprinkle with the chives, and serve immediately.

Asado beef ribs with salsa roja

SERVES 4

SALSA ROJA
6 tomatoes, roughly chopped
2 garlic cloves, crushed
2 jalapeño, stems removed, roughly chopped
1 tablespoon extra-virgin olive oil
salt, to taste
apple-cider vinegar, to taste
1 white onion, finely diced
½ bunch coriander (cilantro), including stems
  and roots, washed

BEEF RIBS
8 × 140 g/5 oz asado beef ribs
salt and pepper, to season

Asado is a beef short rib cut across the bones that is typically found in Argentina where it is cooked on the iconic parrilla grill. Salsa roja is a Mexican staple condiment often served with asado, as we have here, but it goes with pretty much everything!

To make the salsa roja

Put the tomatoes, garlic and jalapeño in a blender and purée to a smooth paste. Transfer to a large saucepan over a medium heat, add olive oil and bring the paste to a boil. Remove from heat and season to taste with salt and apple-cider vinegar. Set aside to cool to room temperature.

Once it has cooled, mix in onion and coriander. The salsa will keep in an airtight container in the fridge for up to 2 weeks.

To cook the ribs

Prepare your charcoal barbecue for grilling (a gas barbecue can also be used, but the flavour imparted by the charcoal method is superior). Light your charcoal – it should take about 15 minutes. Season the asado ribs on both sides with salt and pepper.

Spread your coals out into a nice even bed. You will want them to be hot but spread out into an even layer. The fat from the ribs can cause flare-ups, so you want to minimise hot spots.

Working in two batches, place 4 of the ribs over the hot coals. Cook for 2 minutes, flip the ribs. Cook for a further 2 minutes. Flip them again, and cook for a further 1–2 minutes until cooked to medium-well (they should retain a hint of pink). Remove from the barbecue and set aside to rest for 5–10 minutes. Repeat with the remaining beef ribs.

Cut between the bones into individual ribs and arrange on a serving plate. Season with a pinch of salt and spoon generous amounts of salsa roja over the top to serve.

Cos lettuce with ranch dressing and mint

SERVES 4

A simple salad that is fresh and crisp. Easy to prepare and always delicious.

3 small heads of cos (romaine) lettuce
1 portion Ranch dressing (page 243)
1 small white onion, finely sliced into rings on a mandoline
½ bunch mint, leaves picked

Quarter the lettuce heads, rinse well and leave to drain, or spin dry in a salad spinner. Arrange the lettuce wedges on a serving plate. Spoon the ranch dressing over the lettuce and top the salad the sliced onion and mint leaves.

Potatoes cooked in coal

SERVES 6

The humble potato cooked in the coals of your open fire is about as comforting as it gets. The result is crispy golden skin with a soft buttery interior. You can't go wrong with lashings of butter and a sprinkle of salt, but for something different, we season ours with creamy stracciatella, an Italian cheese made from mozzarella curds, and salty, crispy toasted saltbush.

6 large potatoes (we love yukon gold)
250 g (9 oz) unsalted butter, softened
½ bunch saltbush (see Glossary, page 247)
300 g (10½ oz) stracciatella
salt, to season
chives, finely chopped, to garnish (optional)

Light a good amount of coals or charcoal in your fire or barbecue – you will need enough to bury the potatoes. Using the point of a knife, prick the potatoes all over. Rub them all over with butter, then wrap each of them in a double layer of aluminium foil.

Bury the potatoes in the hot coals and cook for 40 minutes. Unwrap potatoes to check if they're done – they should be crispy on the outside and soft in the centre. If not, continue to cook until done.

A few minutes before the potatoes are ready, cook the saltbush over the coals for a few minutes, or until crispy.

Just before serving, open the hot potatoes, cut in half and season with a pinch of sea salt. Arrange the potatoes on a platter cut side up and place a large spoonful of stracciatella on each potato half. Finish the baked potatoes with a few pieces of crisp salt bush leaves and a sprinkling of chives, if using.

COMFORT

FOOD

A perfect roast chicken

SERVES 4

CHICKEN

120 g (4½ oz) unsalted butter,
    at room temperature
pinch of salt
size 16 (1.6 kg/3½ lb) chicken,
    at room temperature
½ lemon
sea salt, to serve

PAN-JUICE GRAVY

roasting juices from your cooked chicken
1 tablespoon plain (all-purpose) flour
20 g (¾ oz) unsalted butter
125 ml (4 fl oz/½ cup) water
salt and pepper, to season

GEORGIAN FIVE-SPICE (OPTIONAL)

2 teaspoons fenugreek seeds
2 bay leaves
1 tablespoon ground coriander
1 tablespoon dried savory or thyme
1½ teaspoons dried dill
½ teaspoon black pepper
½ teaspoon salt

Combine ingredients in a spice grinder, mill or mortar and grind to a fine powder. Store in an airtight container or jar for up to 6 months.

This is the recipe we use when roasting a chicken at home, and includes the all-important step of removing the wishbone before you roast the bird. It's quite a simple manoeuvre and makes the chicken super easy to carve. Leave the chicken uncovered in the fridge overnight for the best crispy skin.

To cook the chicken

Place the butter in the bowl of a stand mixer fitted with the paddle attachment (or whisk by hand), season with salt and mix on a medium speed until smooth and fluffy, for about 2–3 minutes. Add 1 tablespoon of the Georgian five-spice to the butter, if using, and mix on a medium speed until the spice is fully combined with the butter.

To identify the wishbone, use your finger to feel around under the skin up through the top of the neck cavity at the front of the chicken breasts. When you feel the wishbone, use a small, pointed knife to cut around the outside of it. Once you have cut as much as you can, without piercing the skin, pull the wishbone out.

Preheat the oven to 220°C (430°F). Place the chicken in a roasting tray. Rub the chicken all over with the whipped butter, being very liberal (though any leftover butter can go into the cavity). Put the lemon inside the cavity then truss the chicken legs by tying the drumsticks together with twine so they are tight against the body. Roast the chicken breast-side up for 45 minutes, then turn the oven off and leave the chicken in the oven for 20 minutes or until the internal temperature in the thickest part of the leg is 64°C (145°F). Remove the chicken from the tray, reserving the roasting juices, and rest, covered, for 15 minutes.

To make the pan-juice gravy

Transfer the roasting juices from the tray to a medium saucepan, scraping any caramelised bits from the bottom. Mix the flour and butter in a small bowl. Add the water to the pan juices and bring to a gentle simmer over a medium heat. Add the flour and butter mixture and whisk until the sauce thickens and there are no lumps, about 2–3 minutes. If the gravy begins to split, add a splash of water, remove from the heat and continue to whisk. Season to taste.

To serve

To carve the chicken, remove the lemon from the cavity and cut down either side of the breasts; they will come away effortlessly. Remove the legs and cut in half through the joints (return to a hot oven for a few minutes if they are a touch pink). Arrange the chicken portions on a serving platter and squeeze the lemon half over to dress. Drizzle over the pan-juice gravy and sprinkle with sea salt.

Braised rabbit pot roast with dijon mustard, tarragon and shallots

SERVES 4

1.5 kg (3 lb 5 oz) farmed rabbit
125 g (4½ oz) good-quality dijon mustard
2 tablespoons olive oil
40 g (1½ oz) salted butter
10 golden shallots, sliced
200 ml (7 fl oz) dry white wine
500 ml (17 fl oz/2 cups) chicken stock
1 bay leaf
5 each thyme sprigs and parsley sprigs,
    tied together with butcher's twine
125 ml (4 fl oz/½ cup) crème fraîche
pinch of white pepper
5 sprigs tarragon, leaves picked and
    roughly chopped
salt and pepper, to season
potato gratin and simple dressed butter lettuce
    salad (optional), to serve

We love rabbit. It's as easy to cook as chicken and adds variety to your repertoire. You can use wild or farmed rabbit for this recipe but there are differences. With wild rabbits, the size and meat-to-fat ratio can vary. Farmed rabbits are much more consistent in size and are reliably meaty with a good cover of fat. Your butcher can help you with breaking down the rabbit if you're not quite ready to take that plunge.

Joint the rabbit by removing the rear legs and front runners. With a cleaver or large knife, cut across the saddle into three sections, leaving the fillets connected to the bone. Discard the rib cage. Cut the rear legs in half. Rub half of the mustard onto the rabbit pieces and season with salt and pepper.

Heat 1 tablespoon of the oil and 20 g (¾ oz) of the butter in a heavy cast-iron pan or flameproof casserole dish. Add the shallot and cook over a medium heat until golden, for about 5 minutes. Remove from the pan and set aside. Put the same pan back onto the stove without washing it. Heat the remaining oil and butter over a high heat until foaming, then add the rabbit pieces and cook, turning to brown on all sides, for around 10 minutes until golden. Add the white wine and deglaze the pan, scraping the base of the pan with a wooden spoon. Simmer vigorously until reduced by half, then add the chicken stock, glazed shallots, bay leaf, thyme and parsley. Cover the pan with a lid, reduce the heat to medium-low and cook gently for 30–40 minutes, turning the rabbit pieces from time to time. Remove from the heat and rest for 15 minutes.

Transfer the rabbit to a plate and cover with aluminium foil to keep warm. Discard the bay leaf and thyme and parsley from the braising liquid, then bring to the boil over a high heat and cook until reduced to about 250 ml (8½ fl oz/1 cup). Whisk in the crème fraîche, white pepper, tarragon and remaining mustard. Taste, and season with salt and pepper if needed. Return the rabbit to the pan and serve with potato gratin and a simply dressed butter lettuce salad.

Osso buco with risotto Milanese

SERVES 4

OSSO BUCO

1 kg (1 lb 3 oz) veal shank, cut into 2 cm
  (¾ in) thick slices
50 g (1¾ oz/⅓ cup) plain (all-purpose) flour
1 tablespoon olive oil
40 g (1¼ oz) unsalted butter
1 onion, finely diced
2 garlic cloves, finely chopped
1 celery stalk, finely diced
1 carrot, finely diced
2 anchovy fillets
1 tablespoon baby capers, rinsed and
  squeezed dry
1 bay leaf
200 ml (7 fl oz) white wine
1 litre (34 fl oz/4 cups) chicken stock

GREMOLATA

1 garlic clove, finely chopped
finely grated zest of 1 lemon
3 tablespoons flat-leaf (Italian) parsley leaves,
  finely chopped

RISOTTO MILANESE (SAFFRON RISOTTO)

700 ml (23½ fl oz) good-quality chicken stock
80 g (2¾ oz) diced unsalted butter
1 tablespoon olive oil
½ onion, finely diced
200 g (7 oz) vialone nano rice (see Glossary,
  page 247)
splash of white wine
good pinch of saffron
90 g (3 oz) grated Grana Padano
salt, to season

What can you say about osso buco that hasn't been said before? It ticks every single box. Cook the osso buco the day before you're planning to serve it to develop the flavour. We would also suggest doubling this recipe for the best pasta sauce a few days later.

To make the osso buco

Preheat the oven to 140°C (285°F). Dredge the pieces of veal by rolling them in the flour, then shake each piece with vigour to remove any excess flour. Melt the oil and 20 g (¾ oz) of the butter in a large heavy-based, ovenproof saucepan over a medium heat. Add the veal in batches and seal on each side, cooking until light golden. Set aside.

Using the same pan, cook the onion, garlic and remaining butter over a medium heat until soft, for about 2–3 minutes. Add the remaining vegetables, anchovies, capers, bay leaf and white wine and bring to a simmer. Cook until the wine has reduced by half, for about 3–4 minutes. Return the veal to the pan and add enough chicken stock to cover (if there isn't quite enough stock, add some water so the veal is covered). Bring to a simmer, then place a piece of baking paper, large enough to cover, on the surface of the liquid. Transfer to the oven and cook for up to 2 hours or until the meat is just falling off the bone. Remove from the oven and rest for 30 minutes (this is the best time to cook the risotto if you're making this whole meal on the same day).

To make the gremolata

While the osso buco is cooking, mix all the ingredients together and set aside.

To make the risotto

Heat the stock in a saucepan. Melt half the butter with the olive oil in a different saucepan over a medium-low heat, then add the onion and cook until soft. Stir in the rice until coated with the hot oil. Add the wine, stirring as it reduces, then add 250 ml (8½ fl oz/1 cup) of the hot stock and the saffron. Stir the rice frequently as it continues to cook and absorb the stock, adding more stock as it absorbs. Once most of the stock has been added, taste the rice; it should be al dente, but if you prefer a softer grain, keep adding the stock until it is all used. Remove from the heat and add the remaining butter and parmesan, stirring well to melt the butter. Season with salt to taste. The risotto should be quite wet at this stage, like porridge, but if not, you can use a little hot water to loosen it up.

To serve

If you prepared the osso buco in advance, return it to the oven for 15 minutes to heat through. Sprinkle the gremolata over the osso buco and serve with the risotto.

Corned beef and colcannon
with caper and parsley sauce

SERVES 6

1.5 kg (3 lb 5 oz) corned wagyu brisket
80 g (2¾ oz/⅓ cup) soft brown sugar
2 bay leaves
½ bunch thyme
1 onion, skin on and cut in half

COLCANNON
1.2 kg (2 lb 10 oz) roasting potatoes, skin on
150 g (5½ oz) salted butter
250 g (9 oz) Savoy cabbage, sliced
extra-virgin olive oil, as required
150 ml (5 fl oz) milk
125 ml (4 fl oz/½ cup) pouring (whipping) cream
6 spring onions (scallions), finely sliced
salt and white pepper, to season

CAPER AND PARSLEY SAUCE
1 bunch flat-leaf (Italian) parsley, leaves picked
1 bunch spring onions (scallions), trimmed and
  roughly chopped
1 soft-boiled egg, peeled
4 garlic cloves, chopped
2 tablespoons capers, rinsed and squeezed dry
10 cornichons
3 tablespoons red wine vinegar
185 ml (6 fl oz/¾ cup) extra-virgin olive oil
salt and freshly ground black pepper, to season

We prefer to use a wagyu brisket for our corned beef. The marbling brings a full flavour and terrific texture and prevents it from drying out. To prove that it's possible for the English and the Irish to get along, we've gone Irish with the potatoes. They are a traditional colcannon mash, with soft cabbage folded through the buttery, creamy potatoes – like a big group hug. You will need a potato ricer for this recipe.

Place the corned beef in a large saucepan and cover it with cold water, filling the pot to three-quarters full. Add the brown sugar, bay leaves, thyme and onion. Bring to a simmer over a low heat, then cover with a lid and cook for 2.5–3 hours or until the beef easily pulls away with a pair of tongs. Remove from the heat and set aside to cool. While it's resting, make the other components of the dish.

To make the colcannon
Put the potatoes in a large saucepan of salted water over a high heat and simmer for about 20 minutes or until soft when pierced with the point of a knife. Drain the potatoes, return to the pan and cover with a lid to keep warm.

Meanwhile, melt 50 g (1¾ oz) of the butter in a frying pan over a medium-low heat then cook the cabbage until tender and wilted but not caramelised, for about 3–4 minutes, adding a little olive oil if it feels a bit dry. Season with salt and set aside.

Warm the milk, cream and remaining butter in a saucepan over a medium heat until the butter has melted, then remove from the heat. Using your fingers, peel the warm potatoes, cut into quarters and pass them through a ricer into a saucepan. Fold in the warm milk mixture until combined, then stir in the cabbage and spring onion. Season with salt and white pepper and keep warm.

To make the caper and parsley sauce
Add all the ingredients to a food processor and pulse until roughly combined, then blend until smooth, for about 1 minute. Season with salt and pepper. This will keep in an airtight container refrigerated for 1 week.

To serve
Remove the corned beef from the water, then slice and place on serving plates with the colcannon. Spoon over the caper and parsley sauce to serve.

Boston butt, Parker House rolls, pickles and mustard greens

SERVES 8–10

PARKER HOUSE ROLLS

12 g (¼ oz) dried yeast
375 ml (12½ fl oz/1½) cups water
1½ teaspoons sugar
375 ml (12½ fl oz/1½ cups) milk
2¼ teaspoons salt
75 g (2¾ oz) unsalted butter at room temperature, diced, plus 80 g (2¾ oz) melted butter, to brush the tins
1.1 kg (2 lb 7 oz) plain (all-purpose) flour, plus extra for dusting
2 eggs, plus 2 egg yolks, lightly whisked, for brushing
10 ml (¼ fl oz) vegetable oil

BOSTON BUTT PORK

2 tablespoons smoked paprika
1 tablespoon salt
1 tablespoon garlic powder
1 tablespoon onion powder
1 tablespoon mustard powder
1 tablespoon ground cumin
1 tablespoon ground coriander
1 teaspoon ground white pepper
3–4 kg (6 lb 10 oz–8 lb 13 oz) Boston butt pork shoulder, skinless
1 litre (34 fl oz/4 cups) chicken stock

TO SERVE

salt, to season
1 bunch mustard greens (see Glossary, page 247), large stems removed
Quick jalapeño hot sauce (see recipe, right)
Pickled red onions (see recipe, right)

Contrary to what the name might suggest, Boston butt comes from a portion of the shoulder that includes the blade bone. It's perfect for slow roasting. You don't have to make your own Parker House rolls for this (you could substitute small brioche dinner rolls or bao) but it's totally worth it for the complete experience.

To make the Parker House rolls

Place the yeast in a small bowl with the water and sugar. Set aside. Warm the milk in a small saucepan over low heat, add the salt and butter and heat until melted. Place the flour in the bowl of a stand mixer fitted with the dough hook, then add the eggs, the activated yeast and the butter and milk mixture. Mix on medium speed until combined. Cover the bowl with a damp tea (dish) towel and set aside in a warm place for 10 minutes to rest. Turn the dough out onto a floured surface and knead for a few minutes, then shape into a ball. Brush a large bowl with a little bit of oil, place the ball in the bowl and cover with the tea towel. Set aside in a warm spot for about 2–3 hours, or until it has doubled in size.

Preheat the oven to 180°C (360°F). Brush the inside of two round 27 cm (10¾ in) baking tins with the melted butter. On a floured surface, roll the dough into a rectangle. Cut the rectangle into 4 long strips, then cut each strip into 8 portions, giving you 32 portions. Roll each portion into a ball and place 16 balls into each tin. Brush the balls with the egg yolk, cover with the tea towel and set aside for 30 minutes to prove.

Bake the dough for 35–40 minutes or until golden, then set aside to cool slightly.

To make the Boston butt pork

Preheat the oven to 200°C (390°F). Mix all the dry ingredients in a bowl then rub all over the pork to coat. Place in a large (12 litre/2.6 gallons) ovenproof dish and pour the chicken stock around the pork. Cook for 20 minutes, then remove from the oven and cover with aluminium foil. Reduce the oven temperature to 140°C (285°F), return to the oven and cook for 4 hours. Remove the foil and cook for a further 1 hour, or until the pork pulls away easily with a pair of tongs. Cover with foil until ready to serve.

To serve

If required, warm the rolls in the oven at 100°C (210°F) for 10 minutes. Unwrap the pork, pull apart into chunks and season with salt. Cut rolls in half and fill with mustard greens, pork, hot sauce and pickled red onions.

132

PICKLED RED ONIONS

60 ml (2 fl oz/¼ cup) fresh orange juice
60 ml (2 fl oz/¼ cup) fresh lime juice
60 ml (2 fl oz/¼ cup) fresh grapefruit juice
1 tablespoon red wine vinegar
salt, to taste
2 red onions, thinly sliced

Mix the juices and red wine vinegar together, then add the salt and stir until dissolved. Put the onion in an airtight container and pour over the pickling liquid, then set aside for at least 8 hours to pickle before using. You can keep these refrigerated for up to 2 months.

QUICK JALAPEÑO HOT SAUCE

20 fresh jalapeño peppers, halved lengthways, seeds and stems removed
375 ml (12½ fl oz/1½ cups) apple-cider vinegar
1 tablespoon salt
4 garlic cloves, roughly chopped

Add all the ingredients to a saucepan and bring to the boil over a high heat. Reduce the heat to low and gently simmer for 10–15 minutes, or until the jalapeños are tender. Transfer to a food processor or blender and blend until smooth. Season to taste. Transfer to an airtight container until ready to use. This will keep in the fridge for up to 6 months.

Lamb oyster chops in house marinade

SERVES 4

2 rosemary sprigs, leaves picked and chopped
½ bunch oregano, chopped
30 g (1 oz/1 cup) flat-leaf (Italian) parsley leaves
zest of ½ lemon
2 garlic cloves, sliced
50 ml (1¾ fl oz) fish sauce
50 ml (1¾ fl oz) olive oil
8 lamb oyster chops
mustard, to serve
lemon wedges, to serve

Lamb oyster chops are a cut from the shoulder. They contain terrific intermuscular fat which makes them perfect for barbecuing. To get the full umami romance of fish sauce, marinate the chops the day before you wish to serve them.

To make the marinade, add herbs, lemon zest, garlic, fish sauce and oil to a food processor and blend for about 2 minutes to form a paste.

Put the lamb in a large dish and cover with the marinade, making sure the lamb is coated all over. Cover the dish and leave in the fridge to marinate overnight.

You can cook these in a frying pan, but we think it's best over charcoal. Heat enough charcoal to cook your chops (or heat your frying pan over a high heat), grill (or pan fry) for 4–5 minutes on each side until well caramelised and cooked to medium-well. Set aside in a warm spot to rest for 15 minutes.

Arrange the lamb on a serving platter and serve with the mustard and lemon wedges.

Boudin blanc with white bean braise

SERVES 6-8

INFUSED MILK
100 g (3½ oz) unsalted butter
1 onion, diced
1 celery stalk, diced
2 garlic cloves, crushed
1 carrot, diced
1 bouquet garni (see Glossary, page 247)
1.25 litres (42 fl oz/5 cups) milk
salt and white pepper, to season

BOUDIN BLANC (WILL MAKE APPROXIMATELY 10 SAUSAGES OF 20-22 CM/8-8¾ IN)
830 g (1 lb 13 oz) minced (ground) chicken
30 g (1 oz) salt
5 g (⅛ oz) white pepper
2 g (⅛ oz) saltpetre (see Glossary, page 247)
25 ml (¾ fl oz) Cointreau orange liqueur
20 ml (¾ fl oz) chicken stock
5 g (⅛ oz) porcini powder
1 egg, plus 4 egg whites
½ teaspoon freshly grated nutmeg
15 g (½ oz) plain (all-purpose) flour
10 g (¼ oz) potato flour
zest of ½ lemon
28-32 mm (1-1½ in) hog casings (see Glossary, page 247)

WHITE BEAN BRAISE
400 g (14 oz) small cannellini beans
25 g (1 oz) dried chanterelle mushrooms (see Glossary, page 247)
1 tablespoon olive oil
1 onion, finely diced
1 small leek, top green parts removed and finely diced
2 garlic cloves, finely sliced
1 celery stick, finely diced
100 ml (3½ fl oz) Dry Madeira
700 ml (23½ fl oz) chicken stock
2 thyme sprigs
½ bunch flat-leaf (Italian) parsley, leaves picked and finely chopped
salt and pepper, to season

TO SERVE
mustard

These chicken sausages are a version of the French boudin blanc, which is traditionally a Christmas dish made from pork flavoured with sage and marjoram and mixed with cream or milk. But, just like a puppy, a boudin blanc is not just for Christmas and these are great all year round. You'll need a day or two to make them, and remember to make the infused milk the day before for optimum flavour.

To make the infused milk

Cook half of the butter along with the onion, celery and garlic in a large saucepan over a medium heat, stirring frequently, until the onion is translucent and slightly caramelised. Add the carrot, bouquet garni and remaining butter and cook for 4-5 minutes or until softened. Reduce the heat to low, add the milk and bring to a very slow simmer, then cook for 2 hours to infuse. Remove from the heat and season with salt and white pepper. Once it has cooled slightly, strain into an airtight container and store in the fridge for up to 1 week.

To make the boudin blanc

Pulse the chicken, salt, white pepper and saltpetre in a food processor for about 30 seconds. In a large jug, mix 660 ml (22½ fl oz) of the infused milk with the Cointreau, chicken stock, porcini powder, egg, egg whites and nutmeg. Add the flours to the food processor and blitz for 30 seconds, then slowly add the liquid and blend for about 2 minutes, scraping down the side with a spatula as needed, or until smooth. Transfer to a bowl, fold through the lemon zest using a spatula and put in the fridge to cool.

If you have a sausage attachment on your stand mixer, you can stuff the sausages using this, or you can cut 12 small lengths of hog casing and pipe the mix into the casing using a piping bag. To do this, tie off one end of the sausage casing and pull the open end of the casing over the piping bag nozzle. Gently fill the casing, making sure there are no air pockets and leaving enough of the casing so you can tie off the open end to finish the sausage. Once all the casings are stuffed, store in the fridge for up to 4 days.

To make the white bean braise

Soak the cannellini beans and chanterelles in plenty of water overnight. Heat a large saucepan over a medium heat, then add the oil, onion, leek, garlic and celery and cook for 3-4 minutes, stirring frequently, until softened. Add the Madeira and reduce by half. Drain the cannellini and chanterelles, add them to the pan and cook for 2-3 minutes. Add the stock and thyme, reduce heat to a gentle simmer and cook, partially covered, for 1½ hours or until the beans are tender. Fold through the parsley and season with salt and pepper. Set aside to cool slightly.

To serve

Heat a large saucepan of water over a medium heat until gently simmering. Add the boudin blanc and cook for 30-40 minutes or until the internal temperature is 65°C (150°F). Turn off the heat and leave in the water for 15 minutes or until you are ready to serve. Drain the sausage, slice and arrange on top of the braise. Serve with mustard.

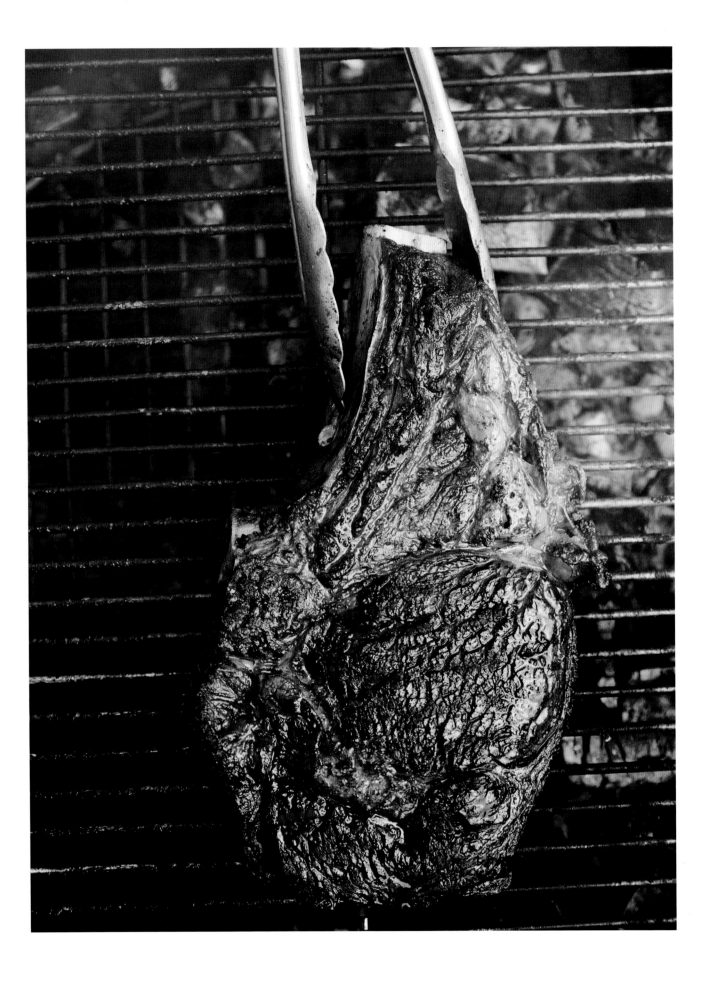

HOW TO GRILL A RIB-EYE, AND THE BEST SAUCES

SERVES 4

Do not be afraid of a rib-eye – it looks tricky but is pretty friendly, once you get to know it. This is an easy, approachable method for that sometimes-daunting grilling challenge and will not only make your fear of stuffing up melt away, but will have people (or even just yourself) crowning you Lord of the Grill. Choose your own adventure with the sauces. Just your favourite? Or all of them?

1.2–1.5 kg (2 lb 10 oz–3 lb 5 oz) rib-eye steak
2 tablespoons olive oil
sea salt flakes, to season

Remove steak from the fridge and allow it to come to room temperature. An hour before cooking, brush the steak all over with a very thin layer of oil and season generously on all sides with salt.

When you're ready to cook, prepare a barbecue for direct-heat cooking. Charcoal is preferred, however gas also works, just ensure you preheat your barbecue to a medium-high heat and follow the same timings in this recipe. To cook over charcoal, light a chimney full of charcoal. Once red hot, add a thin layer of unlit charcoal and pour in the coals – the extra charcoal is to ensure there is enough fuel for the full cooking duration, as well as to elevate the hot coals closer to the grill grate. Replace the grill grate. Ensure the bottom and top dampers are fully open and leave the grill to preheat for 5–10 minutes.

Place the steak onto the grill directly over the hot coals. Immediately place the lid on the barbecue; this will ensure you can cook at a very high heat while choking off enough oxygen to prevent flare-ups. It also ensures the smoke will circulate within the grill, to give the steak a delicious smoky flavour. During cooking, if things are getting too hot or it is flaring up at any time, move the steak to the indirect side of the grill for a few minutes for things to settle down.

Cook for 5 minutes, remove the lid, and turn the steak using a pair of long tongs, then quickly replace the lid. Cook for a further 5 minutes, then turn again, repeating this process a further 2 times, for a total of 20 minutes or until you have a delicious crust on both sides and the thickest part of the steak is medium-rare, with an approximate internal temperature of 48–50°C (120°F). Set the steak aside on a plate, leaving in the meat thermometer, and rest for 10 minutes until the internal temperature is 53–54°C (125°F) for medium (the temperature will rise as it rests).

To serve, use a sharp carving knife to remove the bone. Carve into thick slices and place on a warmed serving plate. Drizzle with oil and season with salt.

Sauces

PEPPER SAUCE

MAKES 840 ML (28½ FL OZ)

450 ml (15 fl oz) grapeseed oil
1 clove garlic, finely sliced
½ golden shallot, finely sliced
10 g (¼ oz) black peppercorns
10 g (¼ oz) white peppercorns
10 g (¼ oz) Sichuan peppercorns
25 ml (¾ fl oz) brandy
115 ml (4 fl oz) balsamic vinegar
40 ml (1¼ fl oz) light soy sauce
50 g (1¾ oz) granulated white sugar
15 ml (½ fl oz) fish sauce
1 litre (34 fl oz/4 cups) chicken stock
4 g (approx. ⅛ oz) xanthan gum (see Glossary, page 247)

Add 45 ml (1½ fl oz) of the grapeseed oil to a large saucepan over medium heat. Once heated, add the garlic and shallot and heat for 3–4 minutes, stirring frequently. Add all the peppercorns and cook for a few minutes until fragrant. Add the brandy and very carefully light with a match to deglaze; once lit, the flames will burn off quickly. Add the balsamic vinegar, soy sauce, sugar, fish sauce and chicken stock and cook until reduced by half, for about 30 minutes. Add the xanthan gum and, using a stick blender, slowly blend to start to emulsify the sauce. After about 1 minute of blending, stream in the remaining grapeseed oil, continuing to slowly blend; you are looking to emulsify in the same way you do mayonnaise (see recipe, page 243). Once the sauce has thickened to your liking, remove from the heat and set aside to cool. This sauce will keep in an airtight container in the fridge for up to 1 month.

CAFÉ DE PARIS BUTTER

MAKES 500 G (1 LB 2 OZ)

500 g (1 lb 2 oz) butter, softened
30 g (1 oz) tomato sauce (ketchup)
15 g (½ oz) dijon mustard
15 g (½ oz) capers, rinsed and squeezed dry
1 large golden shallot, finely diced
25 g (1 oz) flat-leaf (Italian) parsley, finely chopped
25 g (1 oz) chives, snipped
pinch of dried marjoram
5 g (⅛ oz) thyme leaves
5 g (⅛ oz) tarragon leaves, finely chopped
1 garlic clove, very finely chopped
4 anchovy fillets, finely chopped
1 tablespoon brandy
1 tablespoon Madeira
1 tablespoon Worcestershire sauce
½ teaspoon paprika
8 white peppercorns, ground
zest and juice of ½ lemon
zest of ¼ orange
2 teaspoons salt

Add all the ingredients to the bowl of a stand mixer fitted with the paddle attachment and mix on a medium speed for about 5 minutes, scraping the side of the bowl with a spatula, until fully incorporated. Turn out onto a large sheet of baking paper and roll into a log. Twist the ends to close and refrigerate until set, about 2–3 hours. Store any excess butter in the freezer for another day.

DIANE SAUCE

MAKES 500 ML (17 FL OZ/2 CUPS)

80 g (2¾ oz) unsalted butter, diced
2 cloves garlic, finely minced
2 golden shallots, finely diced
160 ml (5½ fl oz) good-quality cognac
180 g (6½ oz) button mushrooms, finely diced
2 tablespoons Worcestershire sauce
1 tablespoon soy sauce
2 teaspoons dijon mustard
300 ml (10 fl oz) thick (double/heavy) cream
60 g (2 oz) flat-leaf (Italian) parsley, finely chopped
salt and pepper, to season

Heat half the butter in a large saucepan over a medium heat until melted. Add the garlic and shallot and cook for about 3–4 minutes until caramelised. Add the cognac and very carefully light with a match to deglaze, keeping your face back from the pan; once lit, the flames will burn off quickly. Add the mushroom and cook for 2–3 minutes, then add the Worcestershire and soy sauce, mustard and cream and cook for 5 minutes or until the sauce is a deep rich colour. Add the remaining butter and remove from the heat, whisking until thickened. Add the parsley and season with salt and pepper. This sauce will keep in an airtight container in the fridge for up to 2 weeks.

RED WINE SAUCE

MAKES 250 ML (8½ FL OZ/1 CUP)

80 g (2¾ oz) butter, diced
8 golden shallots, finely diced
250 ml (8½ fl oz/1 cup) red wine
1 bay leaf
5 thyme sprigs
250 ml (8½ fl oz/1 cup) veal stock
salt and pepper, to season

Add half the butter to a large saucepan over a medium heat. Once melted, add the shallot and cook until soft, for about 4 minutes. Add the red wine and cook until reduced by half. Add the bay leaf, thyme and veal stock, and cook for 1 hour or until reduced by half. Strain the sauce into a medium saucepan and whisk in the remaining butter over a medium heat until fully incorporated. Season with salt and pepper.

BORDELAISE SAUCE

MAKES 250 ML (8½ FL OZ/1 CUP)

2 tablespoons olive oil
1 garlic clove, finely minced
3 golden shallots, finely diced
1 tablespoon brandy
185 ml (6 fl oz/¾ cup) red wine
250 ml (8½ fl oz/1 cup) veal stock
40 g (1½ oz) butter
100 g (3½ oz) beef bone marrow, diced
salt, to season
5 g (⅛ oz) Aleppo pepper (see Glossary, page 247), to season

Add the olive oil to a large saucepan over a medium heat. Once heated, add the garlic and shallot, and cook until translucent, for about 2 minutes. Add the brandy and very carefully light with a match to deglaze; once lit, the flames will burn off quickly. Add the red wine and cook until reduced by three-quarters. Add the veal stock and cook over a medium heat until reduced by half, for about 30 minutes. Remove from the heat, then whisk in the butter and bone marrow until the sauce thickens. Season with salt and Aleppo pepper.

BÉARNAISE SAUCE

MAKES 200 ML (7 FL OZ)

80 g (2¾ oz) unsalted butter
2 golden shallots, finely diced
2 teaspoons white wine vinegar
2 teaspoons lemon juice
2 large egg yolks
60 ml (2 fl oz/¼ cup) thick (double/heavy) cream
2 teaspoons tarragon leaves, finely chopped
salt and pepper, to season
small pinch of Espelette pepper (see Glossary, page 247)

Melt the butter in a saucepan over a medium heat. Add the shallot and cook for 2–3 minutes until it is soft and translucent. Add the vinegar and lemon juice, turn off the heat and stir together. Mix the egg yolks and cream in a bowl, then slowly whisk into the onion mixture until emulsified and thickened. Add the tarragon, then season with salt and pepper. Add the Espelette pepper. This will keep in an airtight container in the fridge for up to 2 weeks.

SUMMER CUP

LAMB IN THE WOOD OVEN

WOOD-ROASTED ARTICHOKES

CLAMS, BACON AND LOVAGE

ROAST BANANA PEPPERS WITH TROPEA ONIONS AND RICE PILAF

BAKED ZUCCHINI AND TARRAGON

LUNCH
IN THE GARDEN

When I cook at home in summer, nine times out of ten you'll find me outside, cooking in the garden. After spending 30 years cooking in basements and airless, back-corner kitchens, I jump at the chance to get outside and cook over coals in the fresh air whenever I can. More often than not, what I'll be cooking will be coming straight from the garden because that's my other summer passion: growing vegetables. If it's in the garden, you know it'll end up on the grill or in the wood-fired oven. Seasonality and regionality is not just a catchphrase when you're pulling veggies straight from the garden and cooking them immediately.

Working with vegetables I've grown in the garden combined with incredible produce from Meatsmith is my happy place. I love to cook for other people professionally, but I enjoy cooking for family at home just as much. It's one of those 'tree falling in the woods and no one hearing it' scenarios – I like an audience for the food I cook.

ANDREW

Summer Cup

SERVES 6

150 ml (5 fl oz) rosé vermouth
(we use Belsazar)
100 ml (3½ fl oz) Fino Sherry
(we use Gutiérrez Colosía)
200 ml (15 fl oz) Brachetto d'Acqui wine
(we use Braida), or any sweet red vermouth
(see Glossary, page 247)
50 ml (1¾ fl oz) Basil syrup, or to taste
(see below)
Cava or sparkling wine to top up
(approx. 300 ml/10 fl oz)
handful of mint leaves
4 thinly sliced strawberries
2 orange wedges
2 lemon wedges

BASIL SYRUP

10 g (¼ oz) basil leaves
100 g (3½ oz) caster (superfine) sugar

Bring a kettle full of water to the boil then allow
to cool down for 5 minutes – you want water that
is at a temperature of approximately 60–80°C
(140–175°F). Pour 100 ml (3½ fl oz) of the hot
water into an airtight container and add the
sugar and basil leaves. Set aside to cool, then
cover with the lid and refrigerate overnight.
Strain, discarding the leaves.

In a perfect world you would make the basil syrup at least the
day before you want to serve this. A long infusion of the basil
will allow for a softer result, getting the most flavour without
the astringency.

Combine the vermouth, wine and basil syrup in a large glass jug filled with
ice and top up with Cava. Add the mint, strawberry, orange and lemon and
stir to let the fruit disperse evenly. After a few minutes, the wine will start
absorbing the flavour of your fruit and herbs. We highly recommend you
don't skimp on the strawberries as they go terrifically well with the basil.
Pour into ice-filled glasses to serve.

Lamb in the wood oven

SERVES 6

1 lamb forequarter (approx. 2½–3 kg/
    5½–6 lb 10 oz)
extra-virgin olive oil, for drizzling
salt, to season
3 onions, quartered
3 bulbs fennel, quartered, 1 bunch tops and
    fronds reserved
1 garlic bulb, smashed
500 ml (17 fl oz/2 cups) water
handful each of rosemary, thyme and flat-leaf
    (Italian) parsley (and any other hard herbs
    you may have growing in your garden)
3 bay leaves

TO SERVE
salt
lemon halves

This recipe is an indulgence that will elevate any celebration. We use the forequarter, which is the complete neck, shoulder and rib. If you don't have access to a wood-fired oven, a conventional oven will also do the trick.

The day before you wish to cook the lamb, rub the whole forequarter all over with a splash of oil and season with plenty of salt. Refrigerate for a minimum of 10 hours.

Preheat an outdoor pizza oven (or conventional oven, if using) to 220°C (430°F).

Arrange the onion, fennel and garlic on a roasting tray large enough to accommodate the lamb. Pat the lamb dry with paper towel and arrange on top of the vegetables. Add 1 cup (250 ml/8½ fl oz) of water to the roasting tray and place in the oven. There should be enough heat initially to caramelise the skin of the lamb – this should take around 20 minutes.

Open the flue to reduce the heat of the oven to 180°C (360°F). Continue to cook the lamb for 3–4 hours, rotating in the oven occasionally and checking that the vegetables are not burning. If the meat is getting a bit too dark, rest a few pieces of foil over the lamb to stop it from colouring and burning.

After about 3 hours, check the lamb by gently tugging on one of the shanks. If the bone comes away easily it is ready. Arrange the herbs, fennel tops and bay leaves over and around the lamb and return to the oven for 10 minutes.

Remove from the oven, cover with foil and set aside to rest for an hour (this will allow the flavour of the herbs to infuse the meat).

To serve, discard any hard herbs and cut the lamb into large pieces (the meat should easily come apart). Arrange on a platter. Carefully remove the vegetables from the baking tray and arrange around the roast lamb. Serve with extra salt and plenty of lemon halves.

Wood-roasted artichokes

SERVES 4

4 globe artichokes
juice of 1 lemon
60 ml (2 fl oz/¼ cup) extra-virgin olive oil
1 garlic bulb, broken into separate cloves
1 bunch thyme
125 ml (4 fl oz/½ cup) water
1 tablespoon lemon juice
sea salt and pepper, to season

Quite possibly the quickest, easiest and most satisfying artichoke preparation we know.

Preheat a wood-fired oven or barbecue to 250°C (480°F).

If you are using a conventional oven, preheat it to 190°C (375°F).

To prepare the artichokes, trim the tops and peel the stem and base of each until you reach the white centre of the stem (there should be no green skin remaining). Place in a bowl of water with the lemon juice until you're ready to cook.

Just before cooking, slice in half lengthways. Using a small teaspoon, remove the furry centre 'choke' and discard. Pour the olive oil into a small enamel or stainless-steel roasting tray. Lay the artichokes in the tray, cut-side down, and arrange the garlic cloves and thyme on top. Pour 125 ml (4 fl oz /½ cup) of water into the tray, cover with foil and roast for 10 minutes. Remove the foil and cook for a further 10 minutes or until you can pierce the heart of the artichoke easily with a sharp knife. Sprinkle with lemon juice and season with sea salt and pepper to serve.

Clams, bacon and lovage

SERVES 4

1 onion, finely diced
1 tablespoon unsalted butter
200 g (7 oz) smoked bacon, diced into
    1 cm (½ in) pieces
100 ml (3½ fl oz) dry white wine or Sherry
1 kg (2 lb 3 oz) clams (vongole), rinsed
3 tablespoons shredded lovage leaves
    (see Glossary, page 247) or Chinese
    celery leaves
juice of 1 lemon
black pepper, to season

Roll up your sleeves, eat with your hands and mop up the best
bits with crusty bread.

Cook the onion and butter in an ovenproof frying pan or baking dish
over a medium heat for a few minutes until aromatic. Add the bacon and
continue to cook for a few minutes until the bacon has started to render
and colour somewhat.

Add the white wine and clams. Cover with a lid and continue to cook for
a few minutes until most of the clams open, standing guard as they do so.
As the clams start to open, transfer to a serving dish and discard any of the
clams that haven't opened.

Add 2 tablespoons of the shredded lovage leaves and lemon juice to the
pan with the clam juices and bacon. Season with plenty of black pepper
and the remaining lovage. Pour the cooking liquid over the clams to serve.

Roast banana peppers with Tropea onions and rice pilaf

SERVES 4

A paella of sorts, which always seems to taste better when cooked over an open flame. Add a few slices of chorizo if you wish, but it stands alone without.

2 tablespoons extra-virgin olive oil
6 banana peppers (see Glossary, page 247)
10 Tropea, cipollini or pickling onions, unpeeled (see Glossary, page 248)
1 garlic bulb
200 g (7 oz/1 cup) bomba paella rice
500 ml (5 fl oz/2 cups) chicken or vegetable stock
pinch of ground allspice
½ teaspoon smoked paprika
salt and black pepper, to season
juice of ½ lemon

Preheat a wood-fired oven (or barbecue with a lid) to 250°C (480°F).

Rub a few drops of the oil into the peppers and put on a baking tray. Roast until blistered and lightly coloured, for about 5–10 minutes, or char over the coals on a barbecue (grill). Remove from the oven (or barbeque) and set aside until cool. Peel the peppers, reserving the cooking juices, and set aside.

Meanwhile, place onions on a tray and roast for 10–15 minutes or until blackened and easily pierced with a skewer. Set aside until cool, then peel, reserving any cooking juices. Don't wash the vegetables in water to rid them of any burnt bits as these will add a delicious smoky flavour to the rice.

Wrap garlic in aluminium foil and bake for 20 minutes. Set aside until cool then peel and separate the cloves.

To cook the rice, heat the remaining oil in a paella pan or heavy-based baking dish. Add rice and sauté over a medium heat for a few minutes. Add stock and bring to the boil. Add allspice, paprika, and a pinch of salt and pepper.

Reduce to a simmer and quickly arrange the peppers and onion over the rice, and add any cooking juices from the roasted vegetables. Distribute the garlic cloves throughout the rice.

Place the pan in the wood-fired oven, or in the barbecue, closing the lid, and cook for about 10 minutes, checking from time to time. Towards the end of the cooking process you may need a little stock as the rice dries out. When the rice is cooked, season with a squeeze of lemon juice before serving.

Baked zucchini and tarragon

SERVES 4

This recipe is one of those happy mistakes from a tray of zucchini (courgette) that was left in the wood-fired oven too long. We can't get enough of the resulting smash.

4 medium (approx. 180 g/6½ oz) zucchini (courgette), sliced in half lengthways
1 tablespoon unsalted butter
6 large sprigs tarragon, leaves picked and chopped
½ lemon

About 1 hour before the lamb is finished cooking, add the zucchini to the same baking tray to cook. Roast for 20 minutes until completely cooked through and soft.

Remove from the oven and transfer to a bowl. Mash with a fork and season with salt and black pepper. While the zucchini is still warm, add the butter and stir in as it melts. Set the zucchini mixture aside to cool to room temperature. To serve, add the chopped tarragon to the zucchini mixture and season with a squeeze of lemon juice.

TIME   TO

KILL

Game tea

SERVES 6

1 raw duck or pheasant carcass
4 chicken wings
2 tablespoons olive oil
2 onions, halved
1 chicken, cut in half
2 carrots, diced
2 celery stalks, diced
2 leeks, diced
1 garlic clove
bouquet garni (see Glossary, page 247)
½ teaspoon black peppercorns
2 cloves
1 tablespoon dried porcini or cep
  mushroom pieces
200 ml (7 fl oz) dry Madeira
salt, to season

Essentially a clear, bronze-coloured, fortifying consommé-like broth made from game bird carcasses, game tea was historically sipped warm from flasks by hunters out on the wild and windy moors in the United Kingdom. In the absence of a moor, or a hunt, it is completely delicious and equally fortifying sipped from a teacup or glass as a full-flavoured pick-me-up. Spiked with aged Madeira, this refined elixir is a rare delight.

Preheat the oven to 200°C (390°F). Using a large cleaver, remove the duck wings from the carcass and cut these and the chicken wings into 1.5–2 cm (½–¾ in) pieces. Cut the duck carcass into 8 large pieces. Arrange all the bones on a baking tray and drizzle with half of the olive oil. Roast for 20 minutes, turning occasionally, or until a deep golden colour.

Meanwhile, put the onion cut-side down in a frying pan with the remaining olive oil and cook over a low heat for 8–10 minutes or until a deep golden colour.

Put the roasted bones, chicken, cooked onion and all the remaining ingredients except the Madeira and salt into a large stainless-steel saucepan. Hold the ingredients down with your hand and place under a running tap until your hand is barely covered with water. Bring to a boil over a high heat, then immediately reduce the heat to low and simmer for 3 hours, using a ladle to skim off any foam, fat or dark impurities that float to the surface during cooking. Strain the broth and discard the contents except for the chicken (this meat will make a good sandwich the following day).

Pass the broth through a piece of muslin cloth into a saucepan and add half the Madeira. Bring to a simmer over a low heat and season with salt. To serve, ladle the hot broth into warm bowls or cups and add 1 tablespoon of the remaining Madeira to each.

Oxtail Niçoise

SERVES 4

1.5 kg (3 lb 5 oz) oxtail pieces
2 tablespoons plain (all-purpose) flour
80 g (2¾ oz) duck fat, lard or olive oil
2 onions, finely diced
4 garlic cloves, chopped
3 tablespoons grappa
150 ml (5 fl oz) red wine
2 carrots, cut into 1 cm (½ in) dice
1 celery stalk, cut into 1 cm (½ in) dice
40 g porcini mushrooms, soaked in 125 ml
    (4 fl oz/½ cup) water
1 bouquet garni (see Glossary, page 247)
400 g (14 oz) tinned chopped tomatoes
2 tablespoons tomato paste
    (concentrated purée)
pinch of cayenne pepper
1 tablespoon lemon juice
2 tablespoons grated Grana Padano
2 tablespoons chopped flat-leaf (Italian) parsley

Monsieur Jacques Médecin, a former mayor of Nice, published a book called *Cuisine Niçoise* in 1974. In it, he shares many of Nice's classic recipes and carefully details how to construct a true salad Niçoise. One of the best recipes though, hidden among all this Côte d'Azur history, is the recipe for oxtail Niçoise. This is our homage to Jacques. It is delicious with mashed potato, weather permitting, or a large dish of buttered fettuccine.

Preheat the oven to 150°C (300°F). Trim any excess fat from the oxtail pieces and dust lightly with the plain flour.

Cook half the duck fat and half the oxtail in a large enamelled cast-iron casserole pot over a medium heat for 10 minutes, until the meat is golden and has a nice crust. Repeat with remaining duck fat and oxtail. Remove from the pan and set aside.

Add the onion to the pan and cook gently for 6–8 minutes, scraping any caramelised bits from the pan, until soft and golden. Add the garlic and cook for a further few minutes or until the garlic is aromatic. Add the grappa and the red wine and continue to cook until the liquid is reduced by half.

Add carrot, celery, mushroom, bouquet garni, chopped tomato, tomato paste and cayenne pepper. Return the oxtail to the pan and add enough water to barely cover. Bring the braise to a simmer, cover with a cartouche (see Glossary, page 247) and a tight-fitting lid and place in the oven. Cook for 3 hours.

Once cooked, set aside to rest for 30 minutes. Take a piece of oxtail from the pot and test for tenderness, the meat should be soft and giving but not falling from the bone. Taste the braising liquid and add salt if you think it is needed. Remove the bouquet garni.

This cooking process can happily be done the day before you plan on eating, as you can simply reheat the next day.

Just before serving, stir in the lemon juice, then sprinkle with Grana Padano and parsley. Return the pot to the oven to warm through for 15 minutes. When ready, place the pot of oxtail on the table and serve straight from the pot – rustic tableside ceremony is our favourite way to eat in any setting, especially at home.

Salt-baked chicken

SERVES 4

size 18 (1.8 kg/4 lb) chicken
2 tablespoons Shaoxing rice wine
2 cm (¾ in) piece fresh ginger, thinly sliced
2 golden shallots, halved
½ lemon
1 tablespoon ground ginger
½ teaspoon white pepper
2 teaspoons salt
2 kg (4 lb 6 oz) rock salt
steamed rice (optional), to serve

GINGER AND SPRING ONION RELISH
1–2 cm (½–¾ in) piece fresh ginger, finely diced
5 spring onions (scallions), thinly sliced
120 ml (4 fl oz) grapeseed oil
1 teaspoon light soy sauce
1 tablespoon sesame oil
1 teaspoon salt

This recipe uses an incredible cooking technique Andrew first came across in Hong Kong, where chickens are baked streetside in paper bags and buried in salt. A good-quality free-range chicken with yellow fat is very important for the texture of this dish. We recommend using a cast-iron pot for best results.

Preheat the oven to 220°C (430°F). Rinse the chicken under cold water, then pat it dry with paper towel and set aside to come to room temperature. Brush the chicken with the rice wine, then put the sliced ginger, shallot and lemon in the cavity. Mix the ground ginger, white pepper and salt, then use to season the chicken all over, also adding a pinch to the cavity. Tie the drumsticks together with butcher's twine. Wrap the chicken twice lengthways in baking paper, then wrap in baking paper twice crossways so the chicken is completely enclosed in paper. Tie the parcel with butcher's twine to secure the paper.

Line a baking tray with baking paper and cover with the rock salt, then transfer to the oven for 15 minutes until hot. Carefully add a 1 cm (½ in) layer of hot salt to the bottom of an ovenproof saucepan large enough to fit the wrapped chicken. Place the wrapped chicken on the bed of salt and spoon the remainder of the hot salt over the chicken so it is completely immersed. Cover with a tight-fitting lid and set aside for 10 minutes, then transfer to the oven and cook for 1 ½ hours. Remove from the oven and rest at room temperature for 30 minutes without removing the lid.

Meanwhile, to make the ginger and spring onion relish, put the ginger and spring onion in a small stainless-steel bowl. Heat the grapeseed oil in a small saucepan over a high heat until 150°C (300°F), then carefully pour over the ginger and spring onion (it will bubble and spit). Stir well to combine, then set aside to cool. Add the soy sauce, sesame oil and salt.

Remove the chicken parcel from the pan, brush away any salt and place in a large serving dish. Using a pair of scissors, open the parcel (at the table for full wow factor). Carefully remove the chicken from the paper and carve. Serve with the ginger and spring onion relish and steamed rice on the side.

Lamb barbacoa

SERVES 5

1.5–1.6 kg (3 lb 5 oz–3½ lb) lamb shoulder
1 teaspoon olive oil
1 × portion Adobo paste (see recipe, below)
2 banana leaves
500 ml (17 fl oz/2 cups) chicken stock

ADOBO PASTE (MAKES APPROX. 1 CUP)
5 cm (2 in) canela (Mexican cinnamon) stick
2 cloves
1 teaspoon black peppercorns
1 teaspoon dried Mexican oregano
¼ teaspoon cumin seeds
4 ancho chillies (see Glossary, page 247),
    split in half and seeded
4 guajillo chillies (see Glossary, page 247),
    split in half and seeded
1 chipotle morita chilli (see Glossary, page 247),
    split in half and seeded
10 garlic cloves, skin on
125 ml (4 fl oz/½ cup) apple-cider vinegar

TO SERVE
10 corn tortillas, warm
1 onion, sliced
1 bunch coriander (cilantro), leaves chopped
Tabasco
12 lime wedges
salt, to season

Note

If you can't find the specific ingredients
for the adobo paste, substitute with a quality
ready-made product.

Barbacoa is a preparation originating from the Caribbean, but
the style of more modern adaptations hails from Yucatán, Mexico.
Traditionally cooked in the ground, we have saved you the effort of
digging a firepit (unless you really want to) by showing you how to
replicate those conditions in your own barbecue at home.

To make the adobo paste

Heat a 30.5 cm (12 in) cast-iron skillet over a medium heat for 5 minutes.
Add the canela, cloves, peppercorns, oregano and cumin and toast, shaking
the pan, until fragrant, for about 15 seconds. Transfer to a spice grinder or
a mortar and grind to a fine powder.

Toast the chillies in the skillet for about 30 seconds, turning from time
to time, until you see the first wisp of smoke. Transfer to a bowl and
cover with hot tap water, then place a heavy plate on top to keep them
submerged. Set aside to soak for 30 minutes. Roast the garlic in the skillet
over a medium heat, turning from time to time, for about 6 minutes or until
softened slightly and blackened in spots. Remove from the skillet and set
aside. When cool enough to handle, peel and discard the skins.

Drain the chilli and add to a blender with the ground spices, roasted garlic
and vinegar. Purée to a paste, adding a little water as needed to help
the chilli pass through the blades. Transfer to an airtight container and
refrigerate until ready to use. The paste will keep for 4 weeks.

To prepare and cook the lamb

Lightly coat the lamb with the oil. Season all over with salt, then cover with
the adobo paste, rubbing it in to ensure it's well coated. Leave to marinate
for up to 12 hours.

Fill a charcoal chimney with coals and pour them into one side of the
barbecue. Fill the chimney again with coals and light them; once they are
white and fully alight, pour them over the top of the unlit charcoal. Adjust
the vents so your barbecue is around 140°C (285°F).

When ready to cook, remove the lid and put a handful of wood chips onto
the hot coals. Place the lamb shoulder on the indirect side of the grill.
Replace the lid and cook for 30 minutes. Remove the lid and add another
handful of coals. Meanwhile, line a flameproof cast-iron pot (30 cm/12 in)
with banana leaves and add the lamb. Wrap the lamb in the banana leaves,
pour the chicken stock into the pot and place the lid on top. Remove the
grill from your barbecue and place the cast-iron pot directly on the coals.
Put enough coals over the pot until it's three-quarters covered. Replace the
lid on the barbecue and cook for a further 2½ hours, topping up the coals as
necessary. Cook until a meat thermometer inserted into the thickest part of
the lamb shoulder reads 96°C (205°F). Rest for 1 hour.

Unwrap the lamb shoulder, remove the bones and shred the meat. Serve in
warmed tortillas with the onion, coriander and Tabasco, with lime wedges
on the side.

Tripe with cuttlefish and 'nduja

SERVES 4

140 ml (4½ fl oz) extra-virgin olive oil

1 kg (2 lb 3 oz) tripe, cleaned of excess fat
and thinly sliced

600 g (1 lb 5 oz) cuttlefish tubes, cleaned
and cut into 1–1.5 cm (½ in) cubes

150 ml (5 fl oz) white wine

1 red onion, finely sliced

4 garlic cloves, crushed

5 thyme sprigs

120 g (4½ oz) tomato paste
(concentrated purée)

2 vine-ripened tomatoes, seeded,
roughly chopped

1 litre (34 fl oz/4 cups) chicken stock

1 teaspoon red wine vinegar

120 g (4½ oz) 'nduja (see Glossary, page 247),
broken into small pieces

salt and pepper, to season

HERB CRUMB

2 slices sourdough bread (approx. 2 cm (¾ in)
thick), crusts removed, roughly chopped

1 tablespoon flat-leaf (Italian) parsley, finely
chopped

1 garlic clove, finely sliced

zest of ½ lemon

Our good friend Chris Watson introduced us to this recipe.
It is a comforting, hearty dish that is full of texture and well
balanced spice.

To make the herb crumb

Preheat the oven to 160°C (320°F). Add the sourdough to a baking tray and
bake in the oven for 15 minutes, or until golden. Let cool, then add to a food
processor along with the parsley, garlic and lemon zest and pulse a few
times until the ingredients are combined. Set aside until needed.

To prepare the tripe and cuttlefish

Heat 2 tablespoons of the oil in a large ovenproof casserole dish over
a high heat. Add the tripe and cook for 5 minutes, stirring regularly;
the tripe will release a lot of liquid. Drain the tripe, discarding the liquid,
and set aside. Clean the dish in preparation for making the braise.

Heat 1 tablespoon of the remaining oil in a large frying pan over a high
heat. Add half of the cuttlefish and season with a generous pinch of salt,
then cook, stirring occasionally, for 2–3 minutes until the cuttlefish is
golden-brown. Deglaze with 50 ml (1¾ fl oz) of the wine, scraping the
bottom of the pan with a wooden spoon. Tip the cuttlefish into a bowl
with any juices and set aside. Wipe the pan and repeat with the remaining
cuttlefish. Set aside.

Heat the remaining oil in the clean ovenproof casserole dish over a medium
heat, then add the onion, garlic and thyme. Season with a generous pinch
of salt and cook over medium heat, stirring occasionally until the onion is
soft, for about 6–8 minutes. Add the tomato paste and chopped tomatoes
and cook, stirring occasionally, for 5 minutes until the tomatoes begin to
soften. Add the tripe, cuttlefish with any of its juices and the remaining
wine. Season with salt and pepper. Add the stock (it should almost cover
the ingredients) and bring to a gentle simmer.

Remove from the heat and top with a paper cartouche (see Glossary,
page 247) to cover the braise. Transfer to the oven and cook for 3 hours
or until the tripe is tender and the sauce is rich and thick. Remove from
the oven, season with salt and pepper to taste, then add the vinegar and
'nduja. Set aside.

To finish and serve

Increase the oven to 220°C (430°F). Top with the herb crumbs and heat
in the oven for 15 minutes to warm through and serve immediately.

Porchetta roast

SERVES 15

1 × 3 kg (6 lb 10 oz) deboned pork belly, skin on
40 g (1½ oz) salt
10 g (¼ oz) black pepper, freshly ground
20 g (¾ oz) chilli flakes or Fermented chilli
  (see below)
10 g (¼ oz) fennel seeds
5 black garlic cloves
zest from 1 lemon
180 g (6½ oz) flat-leaf (Italian) parsley,
  leaves only, chopped
2 tablespoons olive oil
mustard fruits and rocket and parmesan salad
  (optional), to serve

FERMENTED CHILLI

MAKES 1 KG (2 LB 3 OZ)

1 kg (2 lb 3 oz) long red chillies, stems removed
  and roughly chopped
10 g (¼ oz) salt
10 g (¼ oz) caster (superfine) sugar

Pulse the chilli in a food processor for about
30 seconds. Add the salt and sugar and pulse
for a further minute. Transfer the chillies to a
sterilised jar (see note below) and cover with
a muslin cloth. Store in the fridge for up to 1 week
to ferment. The mixture will start to bubble and
become active. Once the fermentation has
slowed, after about 6 days, close the jar with
a lid. Store in the fridge for up to 6 months.

To make chilli flakes, drain off the liquid and
spread on a large baking tray lined with baking
paper. Preheat the oven to 50–80°C (120–180°F).
Cook chilli for at least 6–8 hours or until dry to
the touch. Break it up into small pieces and store
in an airtight container in a dry place for up to
12 months.

Note
To sterilise the jars, bring a large saucepan of
water to a boil over a high heat. Carefully lower
the jars and lids into the water, making sure
the jars are fully submerged. After 15 minutes,
remove the pot from the heat. Remove the jars
and lids and place on a clean kitchen towel to
drain and cool before using.

We like to make our version of porchetta with pork belly, and
it's one of the most popular items we prepare at Meatsmith.
We use belly because we can cook it for a long time so that the
meat breaks down and becomes soft and gelatinous but with
perfectly crisp skin. For the best crackling, we recommend
leaving your rolled porchetta uncovered in the fridge overnight.
This recipe serves a large gathering, but the recipe can be halved
if you're catering for less people.

Start by butterflying the pork belly with a sharp knife, cutting through
the long side of the belly through the middle of the meat, getting as close
as you can to the end without cutting all the way through. Flatten out the
butterflied belly, placing it skin-side down with the meat side closest to
you. Combine the salt, pepper, chilli flakes and fennel and sprinkle evenly
over the whole opened surface.

Peel the black garlic and use the back of a spoon to spread it evenly over
the opened surface. Sprinkle evenly with lemon zest and parsley.

Starting with the part of the belly closest to you, tightly roll up the
meat into a log, so that the skin wraps all the way around. Secure with
butcher's twine in the centre, then at both ends. Then, truss the whole
roast: start at one end and tie a string every two finger widths towards
the middle string. Repeat with the other side. Set aside, uncovered, in
the fridge overnight.

One hour before you are ready to cook, prick the skin all over with the
point of a sharp knife. Rub the porchetta generously with olive oil and
set aside on a wire rack set in a roasting dish. Preheat the oven to
150°C (300°F).

Cook your porchetta, uncovered, for 2½ hours (you can also add
few peeled potatoes to the pan). Increase the oven temperature to
the maximum and continue cooking for 30 minutes until the skin is
blistered and crispy. Once you're happy with the level of crackle on
the roast, remove from the oven and set aside on the bench to rest for
20 minutes. Carve and serve with mustard fruits and a simple rocket
and parmesan salad.

Chicken ballotine, ricotta and grilled peaches

SERVES 4

size 16 (1.6 kg/3½ lb) chicken

CHICKEN STUFFING
300 g (10½ oz) minced (ground) chicken thigh
2 black garlic cloves, finely chopped
   (see Glossary, page 247)
5 g (⅛ oz) Espelette pepper (see Glossary,
   page 247)
5 g (⅛ oz) salt
2 g (⅛ oz) fennel pollen (see Glossary, page 247)
50 ml (1¾ fl oz) pouring (whipping) cream

PAN JUS
2 tablespoons olive oil
50 g (1¾ oz) diced pancetta
bones from your chicken, chopped
50 ml (1¾ fl oz) pastis (see Glossary, page 247)

WHIPPED RICOTTA
250 g (9 oz) ricotta
50 ml (1¾ fl oz) thick (double/heavy) cream
salt, to season
zest of 1 lemon

TO SERVE
2 tablespoons olive oil, plus extra to drizzle
salt, to season
3 large yellow peaches, halved, stones removed
50 g (1¾ oz) pancetta, diced

Based on all our experience with butchery and food preparation, we've come to the conclusion that anything stuffed is always going to be momentous. Learning how to debone a chicken adds nicely to your kitchen skills, too.

To debone the chicken

Place the chicken breast-side down on a cutting board. You should now be looking at the back of the chicken. Using a small sharp paring knife, remove wingettes and tips and set aside. Make a cut along the middle from top to bottom, carefully cutting along the bone all the way around to the breastbone – it will be a little tricky to find the hip joint; twisting the leg will help identify where the right spot is to cut through. Once you have reached the breastbone from both sides, carefully scrape the meat away on either side to find where the end of the cartilage is. Being careful not to break the skin, pull out the chicken frame. Lay the boneless chicken out flat on the cutting board, skin-side down. You will now need to debone the legs. Using the point of your knife, make a cut around the inside of the leg, making sure you are not cutting too deep, only to the depth of the bone. Now do the same around the outside of the leg and, using your fingers, pull the bones away from the meat. You will need to carefully cut around the knuckle joint. Repeat on the other leg, then do the same on the drumettes. Chop all the bones up, including the wingettes, into small pieces and set aside.

To make the stuffing

The stuffing can be made the day before needed. Place all the ingredients in the bowl of a stand mixer fitted with the paddle attachment and mix on a medium speed for 5 minutes, scraping down the side with a spatula every minute or so, until smooth and a little tacky. Cover and refrigerate until ready to use.

To make the ballotine

Place a 45 cm (15¾ in) long piece of plastic wrap on your work surface, then place another 45 cm (15¾ in) long piece in front of it, overlapping by one-third. Repeat so you have 2 layers of plastic wrap in the same positions.

Lay the boneless chicken skin-side down on top of the plastic wrap, positioning it towards the bottom with the breasts furthest away from you. Detach tenderloins from the centre of the breast and flip out to the side, laying flat. Using your hands, shape the stuffing into a log and place it in the centre of the chicken, running horizontally. It might need a little reshaping to fit the width of the chicken.

Bring the boneless chicken legs to the centre and fold them over the top in a rolling motion. As you are rolling forward, tuck in the sides. Once you have rolled all the way over, shape the ballotine, ensuring the skin is wrapped all the way around. Move the ballotine back towards the bottom of the plastic wrap and roll it away from you, holding onto the plastic wrap to enclose the ballotine. Halfway through the roll, pinch and twist the ends of the wrap to keep a log shape. Once you have rolled it up, holding both ends, roll it away from you a few times so the roll becomes tighter. Tie off one end as close to the chicken as you can, then give the loose end a few more twists so everything is nice and tight before tying it off. Refrigerate until you are ready to start cooking.

To cook the ballotine, add 1 litre of water to a large saucepan or enough until it is three-quarters full, and bring to the boil over a high heat. Once boiling, move the saucepan to the smallest burner and turn it to the lowest heat. Carefully drop the ballotine into the water, partially cover with a lid and cook for 1 hour or until the ballotine reaches an internal temperature of 64°C (145°F). Transfer to an ice bath and cool for at least 20 minutes.

To make the pan jus

Heat the oil in a large frying pan over a medium heat, then add the pancetta and cook for 1–2 minutes. Add the chopped chicken bones and cook, turning frequently, for 15 minutes or until evenly caramelised. Add the pastis to deglaze, then add water so the pan is three-quarters full. Reduce heat to low and simmer undisturbed for 1 hour or until the liquid has reduced by two-thirds. Strain the liquid into a small saucepan and set aside.

To make the whipped ricotta

Put the ricotta and cream in a medium bowl. Season with a pinch of salt, then whisk until light and smooth. Fold through the lemon zest, then refrigerate until ready to use.

To serve

Preheat the oven to 200°C (390°F). Remove ballotine from the plastic wrap and place on a baking tray. Drizzle with oil and season with salt, then cook for 40 minutes. Remove from the oven and set aside to rest, reserving any roasting juices.

Meanwhile, heat the oil in a large frying pan over a high heat and add the peach halves, cut-side down. Cook for 4 minutes or until caramelised. Remove from the pan and set aside. Add the diced pancetta to the same pan, reduce heat to medium and cook until crispy. Add the pan jus and any of the roasting juices from the ballotine, then cook it until it just starts to boil. Remove from the heat and stir well.

Spoon the ricotta into the centre of large serving plate. Slice the ballotine and arrange on top of the ricotta. Spoon over half the sauce, then arrange the caramelised peaches around the dish. Serve the remaining sauce on the side.

Zampone (stuffed pig's trotter)

SERVES 8

4 pig's trotters from the hind leg, deboned
(see note, below)

TROTTER STUFFING
800 g (1 lb 12 oz) coarsely minced (ground)
    pork shoulder
200 g (7 oz) coarsely minced (ground) pork jowl
14 g (½ oz) salt
2 g (⅛ oz) saltpetre (see Glossary, page 247)
2 g (⅛ oz) black pepper
5 g (⅛ oz) caster (superfine) sugar
2 g (⅛ oz) ground cinnamon
3 g (⅛ oz) ground cloves
3 g (⅛ oz) paprika
3 garlic cloves, minced
15 ml (½ fl oz) red wine

TROTTER BRAISE
3 onions, finely chopped
6 garlic cloves, finely chopped
1 leek, trimmed and finely chopped
2 carrots, finely chopped
2 celery stalks, finely chopped

TO SERVE
2 tablespoons olive oil
2 onions, finely diced
4 garlic cloves, finely chopped
2 celery stalks, finely diced
400 ml (13½ fl oz) white wine
500 g (1 lb 2 oz) Puy lentils
salt and pepper, to season
½ bunch flat-leaf (Italian) parsley, finely chopped

Note
Start by de-boning the pig's trotters. Using
a small, sharp-pointed knife, and starting from
the end that is cut, slowly work your knife
down in and around the bone, taking care you
don't pierce the skin. It should roll down the
trotter towards the toes, like rolling your socks
off. Keep working all the way until you get to
the knuckles at the toes. Remove the main
bone – you should be left with the skin and
trotter toes intact. Place back in the fridge
until you are ready to stuff them.

Trust us: you need zampone in your life. This boneless, stuffed
pig's trotter is particularly delicious served with lentils, but the
mixture is multi-purpose. You can use it to stuff a chicken or
prepare a faux cotechino (a coarse, slow-cooked Italian sausage)
by wrapping it in muslin and poaching it.

To prepare the trotter stuffing

Mix all the ingredients in a large bowl. Using your hands, mix until
completely incorporated, and the mixture is tacky in texture.

Using a tablespoon, stuff each trotter with ¼ of the stuffing mixture,
making sure there are no air pockets. Push the mixture down firmly and
once the trotter is just over three-quarters full, fold the remainder of the
skin over to enclose the end of the trotter. Truss the whole trotter with
butcher's twine so that it holds its shape while cooking.

Place the prepared trotters, onion, garlic, leek, carrot and celery in a large,
heavy-based saucepan over a high heat. Fill the saucepan three-quarters
full with water and bring to the boil. Reduce heat to a very gentle simmer
and cook the trotters, uncovered, for 3 hours. Turn off the heat and let the
trotters cool to room temperature in the liquid, about 3 hours.

Using your hands, carefully remove the trotters, reserving the liquid, and
place on a baking tray. Carefully remove the string and wrap each trotter
tightly with plastic wrap. Place on a baking tray and refrigerate overnight
to cool. Strain the cooking liquid into an airtight container and place in
the fridge to use the next day.

To finish and serve

Preheat the oven to 180°C (360°). Heat the olive oil in a large saucepan
(big enough to house the trotters) over medium heat and cook the onion,
garlic and celery for a few minutes until softened. Add the white wine and
cook until reduced by half. Add 2 litres (68 fl oz/8 cups) of the reserved
cooking liquid and bring to a gentle simmer. Cook until the liquid has
reduced by half. Add the lentils and cook gently for a further 10 minutes
or until tender.

Remove the trotters from the fridge and remove the plastic film. Transfer
the cooked lentils into a baking tray large enough to fit the trotters, then
gently place the trotters over the top of the lentils and cover with baking
paper. Place in the oven to cook ever so gently for a further 25 minutes.
Remove from the oven and set aside for approximately 15 minutes to
cool slightly.

Gently remove the trotters, season the lentil mixture with salt and pepper,
add the parsley and stir to combine. To serve, slice the trotters, spoon
the lentils into a large serving dish, and arrange the sliced trotters on top.
Finish with freshly-cracked black pepper. This is best eaten warm and is
equally good served with mashed potatoes.

Last night's roast chicken pie

SERVES 4

BONE MARROW PASTRY

500 g (1 lb 2 oz/2 cups) self-raising
(self-rising) flour
1 teaspoon baking powder
½ teaspoon chopped thyme leaves
100 g (3½ oz) unsalted butter, chilled and grated
100 g (3½ oz) bone marrow, suet (see Glossary,
page 247), or butter, chilled and grated
250 ml (8½ fl oz/1 cup) milk
120 ml (4 fl oz) hot water, boiled and left to
cool for 5 minutes
softened butter, to grease
sea salt and freshly ground black pepper,
to season

PIE FILLING

2 tablespoons olive oil
100 g (3½ oz) smoked bacon, diced
1 leek, white part only, roughly chopped
approx. 500 g (1 lb 2 oz) last night's cooked
chicken, meat removed from the bones
700 ml (23½ fl oz) chicken stock
100 g (3½ oz) unsalted butter, diced
100 g (3½ oz) plain (all-purpose) flour,
plus extra for dusting
2 tablespoons soy sauce
salt and pepper, to season
80 g (2¾ oz) sorrel, trimmed of thick stems
(see Glossary, page 247)

TO ASSEMBLE

4 egg yolks, whisked

As a habit, when roasting chicken for dinner we will always roast a second or at least double what is needed. Leftover roast chicken the next day is essential and never ever wasted – whether the meat goes into a pie, is used in a salad or simply shredded to make an incredible sandwich. After you've removed the meat from the carcass, you can use the carcass to make stock. For this pie, make the pastry the day before needed; it's a hot-water pastry that incorporates bone marrow, making it rich, silky and super delicious, and worth the effort. If you'd prefer, you can replace the bone marrow pastry with good-quality store-bought puff pastry; you'll need approximately 750 g (1 lb 11 oz).

To make the pastry (the day before needed)

Put the flour and baking powder in the bowl of a stand mixer fitted with the dough hook attachment and mix on low speed until well combined. Add the thyme and season with a good amount of pepper, then mix for 30 seconds. Add the butter and bone marrow and mix until it resembles breadcrumbs. With the mixer running on a medium speed, add the milk and the hot water and mix until the dough comes together. Turn out onto a floured surface and knead for a few minutes, then place in an airtight container or wrap in a damp tea (dish) towel and refrigerate overnight. Turn out onto a floured surface and roll into a large 5 mm-thick sheet. Grease a 24 cm (9½ in) pie tin that is approximately 5 cm (2 in) high with butter and line with pastry, using the overhang to re-roll and cut a suitable lid. Return the pastry to the fridge to make sure it is really cold.

To make the pie filling

Heat the oil in a large saucepan over a medium heat, then add the bacon and cook until crispy. Remove and set aside. Add the leek and cook for 2–3 minutes or until translucent, then add the cooked chicken and cook for 30 seconds. Add the stock and return the bacon to the pan, then bring to a low simmer and cook for 30 minutes.

Combine the butter and flour then add to the pan and cook, stirring, until well combined and thickened. Remove from the heat, add soy sauce and season with salt and pepper. Once cooled, fold through the sorrel and set aside to cool completely.

To assemble

Preheat the oven to 190°C (375°F). Spoon the pie filling into the chilled pastry base, then brush a little whisked egg around the edge of the pastry. Cover with the pastry lid, joining at the edge by using a fork to crimp all the way around the edge of the pie. Make two small cuts in the middle of the pastry lid to help steam escape while cooking, then brush all over with the whisked egg.

Cook for 25 minutes, then reduce heat to 150°C (300°F) and cook for a further 30 minutes or until the pastry is dark golden. Rest for 10 minutes before serving.

Grilled ox tongue
with anchovy sambal and curry leaf

SERVES 6–8

ANCHOVY SAMBAL
8 dried red chillies
2 fresh red chillies
3 garlic cloves
1 onion, roughly chopped
1 teaspoon shrimp paste
20 g (¾ oz) dried anchovy fillets
3 tablespoons peanut oil
150 ml (5 fl oz) water
2 teaspoons tamarind paste
3 teaspoons sugar
½ teaspoon salt, plus extra, to season

BRAISED TONGUE
1 (approximately 1.6 kg/3½ lb) pickled
    ox tongue
55 g (2 oz/¼ cup) firmly packed soft
    brown sugar
2 bay leaves
4 cloves

TO SERVE
olive oil, to brush
4 tablespoons grapeseed oil
1 bunch curry leaves
salt, to season

Call your butcher ahead of time to organise your pickled ox tongue; tongue is not exactly rare, but many butchers won't just have it as a rule of thumb.

To make the anchovy sambal

Soak the dried chillies in warm water for 5 minutes to soften, then drain. Blend the dried and fresh chillies, garlic, onion, shrimp paste and dried anchovies in a food processor to form a paste. Heat the oil in a small saucepan over a medium heat, then add the paste and cook for 6 minutes, stirring, until the colour darkens slightly. Mix in the water, tamarind paste, sugar and salt. Cook, stirring, for 10 minutes or until the mixture is thick and most of the liquid has reduced. Season with salt and store in an airtight container in the fridge.

To prepare the braised tongue

Put the pickled tongue in a large saucepan and fill with water until three-quarters full. Add the sugar, bay leaves and cloves and bring to a gentle simmer over a medium heat. Cover with a lid, reduce the heat to low and simmer for 4 hours or until the meat pulls away easily with a pair of tongs. Remove from the heat and leave in the liquid until cool enough to handle.

Place the tongue on a cutting board. Remove the skin by pulling it away; you want to make sure the tongue is kept intact, so take your time. Refrigerate until cooled completely.

To serve

Cut the tongue lengthways into thick slices and season with salt. Brush with a little olive oil and season with salt. Heat half of the grapeseed oil in a large skillet pan over a high heat, then add the tongue and cook for 3 minutes on each side or until golden and caramelised. Set aside to rest. Keeping the pan over high heat, add the remaining grapeseed oil and cook the curry leaves until coloured and crispy; they will crack, pop and splatter and cook very quickly, so make sure you are monitoring them closely, this should only take about 15 seconds. Remove from the pan and drain on paper towel.

Serve the cooked tongue on a large serving platter, spoon over the anchovy sambal and arrange the curry leaves on top.

Beef Wellington

SERVES 4

olive oil, to brush
700 g (1 lb 9 oz) centre cut piece of
    beef eye fillet
2 tablespoons dijon mustard
750 g (1 lb 11 oz) good-quality puff pastry
6 egg yolks, whisked
1 tablespoon fennel seeds
1 tablespoon coriander seeds
1 tablespoon cumin seeds
salt and pepper, to season

DUCK LIVER AND FOIE GRAS PARFAIT
250g (1 lb 2 oz) golden shallots,
    finely chopped
150 ml (5 fl oz) port
150 ml (5 fl oz) Madeira
100 g (3½ oz) clarified butter
    (see Glossary, page 247)
200 g (7 oz) duck livers and 50 g (1¾ oz)
    foie gras, diced, or 250 g (9 oz) duck livers
4 g salt
pinch of saltpetre (see Glossary, page 247)
2 eggs

SAVOURY CREPES (MAKES 3)
1 large egg
125 ml (4 fl oz/½cup) milk
30 ml (1 fl oz) water
125 g (4½ oz) plain (all-purpose) flour
⅛ teaspoon salt
1 tablespoon olive oil

DUXELLES
30 g (1 oz) unsalted butter
1 golden shallot, sliced
2 tablespoons dry vermouth
300 g (10½ oz) button mushrooms,
    finely diced
½ teaspoon chopped thyme leaves
salt and freshly ground black pepper,
    to season

Anyone who likes to cook meat should have a stab at making beef Wellington at least once in their lives. It's a technical recipe, yes, with a number of elements involved in pulling it all together, but the payoff – should you accept the challenge – is well worth the effort.

To make the duck liver parfait

In a large saucepan over a medium heat, combine the shallots, Madeira and port. Cook gently for about 30–40 minutes, stirring occasionally, until most of the liquid has reduced. Remove from the heat and set aside.

Preheat the oven to 110°C (230°F).

Warm the butter in a small saucepan over a low heat for 15 minutes or until 40°C (105°F).

Place the duck livers and foie gras, if using, in a food processor and blend for 2 minutes or until smooth. Add the salt and saltpetre, then blend for 2 minutes. Add the shallot reduction and eggs, then blend for 1 minute. With the food processor running, slowly pour in three-quarters of the warm clarified butter and blend until combined. Slowly add the remaining warm butter and blend for a further 2–3 minutes or until smooth. Strain the mixture through a fine sieve into a pouring jug and allow to cool slightly. Pour into 3 small to medium-sized ramekins or jars then place them onto a deep baking tray and cook for 10 minutes. Transfer straight to the fridge to chill. The parfait will keep in the fridge for 1 week.

To make the savoury crepes

Put all the ingredients except the olive oil in a blender. Blend for 1 minute or until the mixture is smooth and has no lumps.

Heat half the oil in a 28 cm (11 in) non-stick frying pan. Add one-third of the crepe mixture, tilting the pan so the mixture covers the base, and cook for 20–30 seconds, then flip and cook for a further 20–30 seconds. Repeat with remaining oil and crepe mixture. Set aside to cool.

To make the duxelles

Cook the butter and shallot in a saucepan over a medium heat for 1–2 minutes. Add the vermouth and cook until reduced by half. Add the mushrooms and thyme and cook, stirring frequently, for 20–30 minutes or until the mushrooms are almost broken down to a paste and the liquid has all but reduced. Season the mushrooms with salt and pepper, transfer to a food processor and pulse a few times so that the mixture becomes more paste-like.

To prepare the beef Wellington

Brush the beef with oil and season with salt. Heat a large frying pan over a high heat and brown the beef all over. Transfer to the fridge to cool.

Lay out three savoury crepes next to each other, slightly overlapping, then use a spoon to spread over a thin layer of the duxelles. Then apply about a 3 mm-thick coating of the duck liver parfait over the top of the duxelles. Refrigerate any remaining parfait for another use Brush the cooled beef all over with mustard. Place the beef in the centre of the crepes and roll up and over the beef, tucking the sides in as you roll.

If using a block of pastry roll out a 40 cm × 40 cm (15 ¾ in) sheet of puff pastry or lay out your pre rolled sheets, then brush all over with egg yolk. Place the beef in the middle of the pastry. Fold in the sides – they should only come in about 4 cm (approx. ¼ in) on the beef –, then roll over from the closest point to you to enclose the beef. Once you have made a nice even cylinder roll of pastry, cut away any excess. Brush the whole wellington with egg yolk and transfer to the fridge to cool for 1 hour.

Preheat the oven to 200°C (390°F). Combine the fennel, coriander, and cumin seeds. Place the wellington onto a baking tray lined with baking paper, Brush again with egg yolk and sprinkle liberally, all over, with the seeds and a sprinkle of salt. Cook for 40 minutes, or until the internal temperature reaches approximately 48°C (120°F), then rest for 20 minutes. Resting is important as the residual heat will keep it cooking to reach an internal temperature of approximately 54–57°C (130–135°F), which will stop the juices coming out of the beef when you carve.

We suggest serving the beef wellington with Bordelaise sauce (page 145).

Boudin noir terrine
with green sauce and fried egg

SERVES 12

TERRINE

½ teaspoon ground allspice
pinch of ground cloves
pinch of ground cinnamon
pinch of ground nutmeg
1 pork jowl
½ pig's trotter
200 g (7 oz) duck fat
1.5 kg (3 lb 5 oz) onions, finely diced
2 garlic cloves, chopped
1 golden shallot, chopped
125 ml (4 fl oz/½ cup) Calvados
   (see Glossary, page 247)
1 litre (34 fl oz) pig's blood
35 g (1¼ oz) salt
6 g saltpetre (see Glossary, page 247)
5 g (⅛ oz) black pepper
15 g (½ oz) chervil, finely chopped
30 g (1 oz) parsley, finely chopped
10 g (¼ oz) tarragon, finely chopped
5 g (⅛ oz) thyme, finely chopped

Boudin noir is a traditional French blood sausage. We have applied a traditional method and have used pork jowl and trotter meat to make a terrine that packs a wallop in terms of both texture and flavour. Pig's blood can take some planning to source (many butchers will only get it in once a week, so call ahead), and this recipe involves a couple of days' work, so it won't be the first choice for a quick Monday night dinner. Still, the end product rewards the effort for more adventurous cooks with a bit of time up their sleeves.

To make the terrine

Mix together the allspice, clove, cinnamon and nutmeg. Set aside.

Put the pork jowl and trotter into a large heavy-based saucepan and cover with water. Bring to a simmer over a low heat, then cover with a lid and cook for 3–4 hours or until the meat pulls away from the bone easily with a pair of tongs. Drain and set aside to cool.

Meanwhile, melt the duck fat in a large heavy-based saucepan over a medium heat. Add the onion, garlic and shallot and cook, moving frequently, for 5 minutes until softened but not coloured. Reduce the heat to low, add the Calvados and cook, stirring frequently, for 30 minutes or until fully cooked through and translucent. Set aside to cool in the pan.

Slice the pork jowl into 5 mm (¼ in) pieces and add to this mixture. Strain the blood through a fine sieve. Add this to the meat and fold together using a spatula. Finally, add the onion mixture, spices and chopped herbs and fold in until incorporated.

Line one large (4.5 cm/1¾ in wide × 24 cm/9½ in long × 8 cm/3¼ in deep) loaf tin with baking paper, leaving enough overhang to cover the top. Using a small ladle, ladle the mixture into the tin. Knock the tin on the bench three times to make sure there are no air pockets, then use the overhang of baking paper to cover.

Preheat the oven to 85°C (185°F). Place the tin into a deep baking dish. Fill the baking dish with hot water to one-third of the way up the tin. Transfer to the oven and cook for 1 hour or until the terrine reaches an internal temperature of 70°C (160°F).

Remove the terrine from the oven and cool slightly, then refrigerate overnight to cool completely.

GREEN SAUCE

120 g (4½ oz) rocket (arugula), roughly chopped
100 g (3½ oz) flat-leaf (Italian) parsley,
   roughly chopped
100 g (3½ oz) coriander (cilantro),
   roughly chopped
80 g (2¾ oz) chives, snipped
4 garlic cloves, crushed
125 ml (4 fl oz/½ cup) extra-virgin olive oil
zest and juice of ½ lemon
200 ml (7 fl oz) crème fraîche or sour cream
salt and pepper, to season

TO SERVE

1 tablespoon olive oil
6 eggs

To make the green sauce

Put all the ingredients except the crème fraîche and salt and pepper in a food processor. Blend, scraping the sides with a spatula, until combined. Add the crème fraîche and blend until smooth. Season with salt and pepper.

To serve

Turn out the terrine onto a chopping board, removing the baking paper, and cut into 6 × 2.5 cm (1 in) slices. Heat the oil in a large frying pan over a medium heat, then add the slices of terrine in batches, being careful not to overcrowd the pan, and cook for 2 minutes on each side. Transfer to serving plates. Using the same frying pan, fry the eggs. Place a fried egg on top of each slice of terrine and spoon over the green sauce to serve. Any remaining terrine will keep in a sealed container in the fridge for up to 1 week.

Pork collar chop with sauce charcuterie

SERVES 4

4 pork collar chops
salt, to season (if not brining the pork)
grapeseed oil, to brush

BRINE
1 litre (34 fl oz/4 cups) water
100 g (3½ oz) sea salt
2 bay leaves
zest of 1 lemon
1 teaspoon fennel seeds
1 tablespoon honey
1 teaspoon white peppercorns
4 thyme sprigs

SAUCE CHARCUTERIE
20 g (¾ oz) salted butter
100 g (3½ oz) golden shallot, diced
20 g (¾ oz) garlic, chopped
250 ml (8½ fl oz/1 cup) white wine
3 thyme sprigs
250 ml (8½ fl oz/1 cup) chicken stock
2 tablespoons dijon mustard
1 teaspoon lemon juice
1 teaspoon capers, rinsed and squeezed
  dry, chopped
50 g (1¾ oz) cornichons, thinly sliced into discs
1 tablespoon chopped parsley

A pork collar chop contains all the goodness from various muscles (neck, shoulder, loin) and is packed full of flavour. Meat from pigs with older European pedigrees, such as Tamworth, Berkshire, Hampshire and Large Blacks, is best. Good-quality chops don't necessarily need to be brined, but the brining process does create a juicy, full-flavoured result. We've also used this recipe on a whole butterflied chicken with marvellous results. Prepare the brine the day before.

To brine the pork

Simmer all the brine ingredients in a large saucepan over a medium heat. Remove the brine from the heat, let cool and then refrigerate. A few hours before you wish to cook the pork, place it into a container that will fit the chops snugly, not stacked on top of each other. Strain the brine and pour over the pork, then refrigerate for 2–2½ hours, turning occasionally.

To make the sauce

Warm the butter in a small non-reactive saucepan over a medium heat, then sauté the shallot and garlic until transparent. Add the wine and thyme, then bring to a simmer and cook until reduced by half. Add the stock and reduce until the consistency of a thick glaze. Remove the thyme sprigs and set the sauce aside until ready to use.

When ready to serve, warm over a low heat, then add the mustard and whisk until dissolved. At the last moment, add the lemon juice, capers, cornichons and parsley.

To serve

If you brined your pork, remove from the brine, pat dry and bring to room temperature. If you have not brined your pork, season well with salt and simply bring to room temperature.

Meanwhile, preheat your barbecue grill until relatively hot. Once again, pat dry the pork with paper towel and brush with a few drops of grapeseed oil. Cook the chops on the grill, turning occasionally, for 5–7 minutes or until they reach an internal temperature of 62°C (145°F). Rest for 15 minutes, then return to the grill for 1–2 minutes to warm, turning a few times. Carve off the bone into 1 cm (½ in) thick slices and arrange on a serving plate. Spoon the warm sauce charcuterie over the chops and serve.

CREPES PARMENTIER AND A CAVIAR SERVICE

GLAZED ROAST DUCK WITH MADEIRA SAUCE

CONFIT DUCK

DUCK NECK SAUSAGE

BRAISED PEAS AND LETTUCE

POMME PURÉE

PARSNIP, ORANGE AND VADOUVAN GRATIN

DUCK PARFAIT AND VERMOUTH JELLY TARTS

DUCK PARTY

Duck is my vice and my greatest joy, both to cook with and to eat. It's something that brings me, and most people I know, a lot of satisfaction. It is the one ingredient I love to cook when a celebration is imminent. These recipes are about a sense of occasion: a duck feast. One of the reasons I enjoy duck so much is that it's so versatile and lends itself to more techniques than most birds. You can cook it with salt water or confit it or make sausages, rillettes or terrines. You can roast it, braise it, steam it, curry it, or cure it. Then there's the duck fat, which is liquid gold. And the bones make a great soup. What's not to love in a somewhat borderline-obsessive way? It ticks every single duck box – and that can only ever be a good thing.

ANDREW

Crepes parmentier and a caviar service

SERVES 4

CREPES PARMENTIER

500 g (1 lb 2 oz) all-purpose potato, peeled
    and diced into 1.5–2 cm pieces
50 ml (1¾ fl oz) milk
3 egg yolks
85 ml (2¾ fl oz) pouring (whipping) cream
35 g (1¼ oz) self-raising (self-rising) flour, sifted
salt, to season
4 egg whites
50 ml (1¾ fl oz) clarified butter

TO ASSEMBLE

50 g (1¾ oz) of your preferred caviar
crushed ice
2 hard-boiled eggs, finely chopped
½ bunch chives, snipped
150 g (5½ oz) crème fraîche

These are similar to buckwheat blinis, which are the traditional accompaniment to caviar. The lightness of these little pancakes is a treat with or without the caviar.

To make the crepes parmentier

Put the potato in a small saucepan and cover with cold water. Bring to the boil over a high heat, then reduce the heat to medium and simmer for 8–10 minutes, or until just cooked; take care not to overcook the potatoes or the batter will be too wet. Strain the potato, then pass through a mouli, ricer or use a spatula to push the potato through a fine sieve.

Whisk together the milk, egg yolks and cream, then pour over the potato and stir well. Mix in the flour and season with a pinch of salt. When you are ready to serve, whisk the egg whites with a pinch of salt until soft peaks form, then fold into the potato batter.

Heat 1 tablespoon of the clarified butter in a non-stick frying pan over a medium heat. Add 1 tablespoon of the batter at a time to make small 'pancakes' the size of a 50-cent piece. Cook for 2–3 minutes or until golden on one side, then flip for a moment to finish cooking.

To assemble

Preheat the oven to 180°C (360°F). To serve the caviar, first find a bowl that will snugly hold the tin. Fill the bowl with crushed ice, open the tin of caviar and place on top of the ice. Serve the chopped egg, chives and crème fraîche in three separate bowls. Line a baking tray with baking paper and warm the crepes in the oven for 2 minutes. Serve the crepes parmentier on a plate alongside the caviar and accompaniments.

Glazed roast duck with Madeira sauce

SERVES 4

1 × 1.8 kg (4 lb) dry-aged duck, room temperature
2 tablespoons maple syrup
salt, to season
1 teaspoon fennel seeds, coarsely ground
1 teaspoon coriander seeds, coarsely ground

MADEIRA SAUCE
1 tablespoon grapeseed oil
4 golden shallots, sliced
1 small carrot, cut into ½ cm (¼ in) dice
4 thyme sprigs
5 flat-leaf (Italian) parsley sprigs
½ fresh bay leaf
1 teaspoon peppercorns
200 ml (7 fl oz) Madeira
250 ml (4 fl oz/½ cup) brown chicken stock
    or duck stock

While it's not entirely necessary to use dry-aged duck, it will definitely elevate the dish. Find a specialist butcher that dry-ages meat; at Meatsmith, we age our duck for seven days. The dry-ageing process uses natural bacteria to break down the meat and sinew, and under the controlled environment slowly dissipates the natural water retention. The product at the end of its ageing process is dense in texture and has a deep rich umami flavour. We have also included a recipe for confit duck if you would prefer to remove the legs and confit them.

To roast the duck

Preheat the oven to 190°C (375°F). Prick the duck skin all over with a sharp metal skewer to pierce the skin and fat, being careful not to penetrate the flesh. Brush the duck evenly with 1 tablespoon of the maple syrup and season generously with salt. Place the duck on a wire rack set inside a roasting tray and roast for 15 minutes, then remove and brush the duck with the remaining maple syrup and sprinkle evenly with the fennel and coriander seeds. Roast for a further 25–30 minutes or until the skin is brown and crisp, the internal temperature is 64°C (145°F) and the breast meat is nicely cooked. Rest for 30 minutes. Baste with the pan juices while resting.

To make the Madeira sauce

Meanwhile, to make the Madeira sauce, warm the grapeseed oil in a small stainless-steel saucepan over a medium heat. Add the shallot and carrot and cook for 2–3 minutes or until they start to caramelise. Add the herbs, peppercorns and Madeira and simmer until almost completely reduced. Add the stock and gently simmer for 10 minutes, adding a little water if the sauce reduces too much and becomes too dry. Strain the sauce and return to a clean saucepan.

To serve

Remove the duck legs and return them to the oven for 5 minutes to warm through, then cut them in half. Remove the breasts from the crown and carve each into four even-sized slices. Arrange two slices of the carved duck breast on each plate with either a thigh or a drumstick. Gently warm the Madeira sauce, then transfer to a jug and serve the sauce on the side.

Confit duck

SERVES 8

approx. 630 g (1 lb 2 oz/2 cups) rock salt,
   as needed
8 garlic cloves, smashed
½ bunch thyme sprigs
4 bay leaves
1 tablespoon black peppercorns
8 duck legs
2 litres (68 fl oz/8 cups) duck fat

Quite possibly one of the most useful and delicious meat preparations for any kitchen. A great tool to get ahead of the dinner party game. Some great butchers sell confit duck legs cooked and ready to go – we do! Leftover duck fat should be kept, and used any time you plan on roasting potatoes.

Place the rock salt, garlic, thyme, bay and pepper corns in a food processor. Pulse the salt mixture to break up the rock salt. Place duck legs, skin-side down, on a non-reactive tray and cover the duck legs with half of the salt mixture. Turn each duck leg over and sprinkle with the remainder of the salt mixture. Transfer the duck legs to the fridge to cure overnight.

To cook, rinse duck legs thoroughly, then place snugly into a large saucepan and cover with duck fat. Cook very gently over a low heat for 3–4 hours or until soft and almost falling off the bone. There should be barely any movement in the fat as the legs cook, just a gentle plopping occasionally. The duck will keep in the fat for up to 1 week in the fridge.

When you wish to use the duck legs, preheat the oven to 210°C (430°F). Gently remove the duck legs from the fat, place them skin-side up onto a baking tray lined with baking paper and bake for 20–30 minutes.

Alternatively, reheat the confit duck legs on slices of cooked potato. The potato crisps up nicely and absorbs all the delicious duck fat and juices of the confit meat.

Duck neck sausage

SERVES 4 (THIS RECIPE MAKES ENOUGH STUFFING FOR 1 SAUSAGE)

1 teaspoon ground allspice
⅓ teaspoon ground cloves
⅓ teaspoon ground cinnamon
⅓ teaspoon ground nutmeg
100 g (3½ oz) minced (ground) chicken thigh
100 g (3½ oz) minced (ground) pork belly
5 g (⅛ oz) salt
3 g (⅛ oz) pink peppercorns
10 g (¼ oz) roasted and peeled hazelnuts, crushed
10 ml (¼ fl oz) pouring (whipping) cream
2 g (⅛ oz) thyme leaves
skin of 1 duck neck
1 tablespoon olive oil

A great use for a cut that is usually discarded.

Mix together the allspice, clove, cinnamon and nutmeg.

Using your hands, mix the chicken, pork and salt in a large bowl for about 2 minutes until the salt has dissolved. Add the whole pink peppercorns, crushed hazelnuts, cream, thyme and spice mix and mix for a further 2 minutes until combined. Refrigerate until ready to use.

Turn the duck neck skin inside out and remove any thick fat parts, glands, and any other sinew, taking care not to pierce the skin. Turn the skin inside out again and, at the smallest end of the skin, close the opening with some twine. Roll the neck skin down halfway and use a tablespoon to push the meat mixture into the casing and fill, making sure there are no air pockets. Close off the end with some twine and refrigerate for 30 minutes.

Fill a saucepan three-quarters full with water and bring to a simmer. Carefully lower the sausage into the water and gently simmer for 40 minutes. Remove from the water and set aside to cool in the fridge. Pat the sausage dry, then heat the oil in a frying pan over a medium heat and gently fry the sausage, turning frequently, for 3–5 minutes until it is evenly caramelised and golden. Slice the sausage and serve.

Braised peas and lettuce

SERVES 4

We follow the traditional French preparation here – the addition of mint is the only deviation from the original.

5 spring onions (scallions)
40 g (1½ oz) unsalted butter
400 g (14 oz) fresh peas
500 ml (17 fl oz/2 cups) water
1 tablespoon olive oil
2 cos (romaine) lettuce, halved lengthways
1 teaspoon lemon juice
a few thyme sprigs
handful of mint leaves
handful of flat-leaf (Italian) parsley, chopped
salt and freshly ground black pepper, to season

Slice the spring onions into ½ cm (¼ in) rounds, reserving the sliced green portion for serving. Warm half of the butter in a small saucepan over a medium heat until melted, then add the spring onion and cook for 2–3 minutes until softened. Add the peas and water, bring to the boil, cover with a lid, reduce the heat to low and simmer gently for 5 minutes, stirring occasionally.

While the peas are simmering, heat the oil and remaining butter in a large frying pan over a medium heat. Add the lettuce, cut-side down, and cook for 6 minutes or until well charred.

Transfer the lettuce to a serving platter. Add the lemon juice, spring onion greens and herbs to the saucepan and stir to combine. Remove the thyme sprigs and spoon the peas over the lettuce. Season with salt and pepper. Serve immediately.

Pomme purée

SERVES 4

Does the world really need another recipe for mashed potato? This is ours.

500 g (1 lb 2 oz) boiling (such as desiree) potatoes, peeled and diced
75 ml (2½ fl oz) milk
75 ml (2½ fl oz) pouring cream
150 g (5½ oz) cold unsalted butter, diced
salt, to season

Place the potato in a large saucepan and cover with cold water. Add a good pinch of salt and bring to the boil over a medium heat, then reduce heat to low and simmer for 15–20 minutes until tender. Strain the potato, then pass through a mouli, ricer or use a spatula to push the potato through a fine sieve into a large saucepan.

Meanwhile, pour the milk and cream into another saucepan and bring to the boil over a medium heat. Set aside.

Place the mashed potato over a low heat and, using a small ladle, add some milk and cream to the mash, stirring all the while. Add a few pieces of the diced butter and stir until combined. Repeat until all the butter and milk has been added and the mash is creamy and light. Season with salt to taste.

Parsnip, orange and vadouvan gratin

SERVES 8

500 g (1 lb 2 oz) boiling (such as desiree) potatoes, peeled
1 tbsp vadouvan spice mix (see recipe, below)
600 g (1 lb 5 oz) parsnips, peeled
40 g (1½ oz) unsalted butter, softened
1 large onion, peeled and diced
500 ml (17 fl oz) pouring (whipping) cream
300 ml (10 fl oz) chicken stock
zest of 1 lemon
zest of 1 orange
pinch of ground nutmeg
salt and pepper, to season

VADOUVAN SPICE MIX
2 teaspoons dried curry leaves
¾ teaspoon fenugreek seeds
2 teaspoons ground cumin
2 green cardamom pods
¾ teaspoon brown mustard seeds
¼ teaspoon turmeric powder
¼ teaspoon ground nutmeg
¼ teaspoon chilli powder
4 cloves
1¼ teaspoons garlic powder

Quite possibly our favourite parsnip recipe ever. This pairs so well with duck but would be equally at home next to a good steak.

To make the vadouvan spice mix, blend all the ingredients together in a spice grinder or mortar and pestle. Store in a tightly sealed jar.

Preheat the oven to 180°C (360°F). Using a mandoline, slice the potatoes and parsnips to about 2 mm (⅛ in) thick and set aside in a bowl of cold water.

Brush the base and sides of a 34 × 24 cm (13½ × 9½ in) baking dish with half of the softened butter. Layer the potato, overlapping slightly, followed by a layer of parsnip until the base of the dish is covered. Scatter over some of the onion and season with a little salt and pepper and a sprinkle of vadouvan spice mix. Repeat this process once again, using up all of the potato, parsnip, onion and spice mix. Set aside.

Warm the cream and stock in a saucepan over a medium heat until it just comes to the boil, then pour it carefully and slowly over the gratin. Dot the remaining butter over the top, finish with the orange and lemon zest, dust with nutmeg and cover the dish with aluminium foil. Bake for 1 hour, then remove the foil and increase the oven temperature to 190°C (375°F). Cook for a further 30 minutes or until the potato is cooked, most of the liquid is absorbed and the top has a golden crust. Remove from the oven. For best results, leave the gratin for 1–2 hours to cool to room temperature and set, then warm through in the oven just before serving.

Duck parfait and vermouth jelly tarts

SERVES 8

TART SHELLS
300 g (10 ½ oz) plain (all-purpose) flour,
  plus extra for dusting
2 g (⅛ oz) salt
130 g (4½ oz) cold unsalted butter, diced
85 ml (4½ oz) iced water
vegetable oil, for greasing

VERMOUTH JELLY
50 ml (1¾ fl oz) cold water
3 titanium-strength gelatine leaves
150 ml (5 fl oz) vermouth rouge
1 tablespoon maple syrup
½ teaspoon white wine vinegar

Here's a guarantee: the combination of flaky, almost crumbly, shortcrust pastry with decadent duck liver and foie gras parfait will increase your popularity, whether you offer this tart as a single serve starter or slice it up to offer as a canapé. The rich, dark vermouth jelly will seal the deal.

To make the tart shells

Put flour, salt and butter in the bowl of a stand mixer. Mix on lowest speed until it resembles breadcrumbs. Slowly add the water and mix for 10 seconds, then remove from the bowl and turn out onto a lightly floured bench. Using your hands, mix the dough until completely combined, scraping the dough across the bench with your palm. Wrap the dough in a damp tea (dish) towel and set aside in the fridge for at least an hour.

Preheat the oven to 160°C (320°F) and grease four tart tins with removable bases (9 cm/3½ wide × 2 cm/¾ in deep) with oil.

Roll the pastry out to 5 mm (¼ in) thick and cut out 4 pieces of pastry large enough to line your prepared tart tins. Line each tin with pastry and baking paper and fill with baking beads (or uncooked rice or dried beans). Set aside to rest in the fridge for 20 minutes before baking.

Place the tins on a baking tray and bake for 20 minutes. Remove the beans and continue cooking for 10–12 minutes or until the centre is crisp and golden. Once golden, take it out of the oven and set aside to cool.

To make the vermouth jelly

Place the gelatine sheets in a bowl with the cold water for a few minutes or until soft. Combine the remaining ingredients in a small saucepan over a medium heat, then add the gelatine mixture and bring to the boil. Remove from the heat and set aside to cool.

DUCK LIVER AND FOIE GRAS PARFAIT
250 g (9 oz) golden shallots, finely chopped
150 ml (5 fl oz) Tawny Port
150 ml (5 fl oz) Madeira
100 g (3½ oz) clarified butter
200 g (7 oz) duck livers and 50 g (1¾ oz)
 foie gras, diced, or 250 g (9 oz) duck livers
4 g salt
pinch of saltpetre (see Glossary, page 247)
2 eggs

To make the parfait and to set the tarts

In a large saucepan over a medium heat, combine the shallot, Madeira and Port. Cook gently for about 30 minutes, stirring occasionally, until most of the liquid has reduced. Remove from the heat and set aside.

Preheat the oven to 110°C (230°F).

Warm the butter in a small saucepan over a low heat for 15 minutes or until 40°C (105°F).

Combine the duck livers and foie gras, if using, in a food processor and blend for about 2 minutes.

Place the duck livers and foie gras, if using, in a food processor and blend for 2 minutes or until smooth. Add the salt and saltpetre, then blend for 2 minutes. Add the shallot reduction and eggs, then blend for 1 minute. With the food processor running, slowly pour in three-quarters of the warm clarified butter and blend until combined. Slowly add the remaining warm butter and blend for a further 2–3 minutes or until smooth with no lumps.

Pour the parfait mix into the tart shells, filling them to three-quarters full, and bake for 10 minutes.

Remove the tarts from the oven and set aside to cool slightly, then transfer to the fridge for about 2 hours to cool completely. Once cool, gently warm the jelly and pour it over the parfait, filling to the top of each pastry shell. Return to the fridge for about 1 hour or until set. To serve, remove from the fridge, and gently prise each tart out of its tin. Cut the tarts in half and serve one half per person.

ONE GREAT

DESSERT

Crème caramel

SERVES 6

CARAMEL
160 g (5½ oz) caster sugar
150 ml (5 fl oz) water

CUSTARD
6 eggs
½ vanilla bean, seeds scraped, or ½ teaspoon
    pure vanilla paste
75 g (2¾ oz) caster (superfine) sugar
430 ml (14½ fl oz) milk
300 ml (10 fl oz) pouring (whipping) cream

We've cooked this recipe more than any other dessert. It's our favourite and the recipe never fails. The large format also adds enough wow factor for the end of the night.

To make the caramel

Combine sugar and water in a heavy-based saucepan over a medium heat. Bring to the boil, stirring occasionally to dissolve the sugar. Once dissolved, continue to boil rapidly, without stirring, until the mixture turns golden brown.

Pour the caramel into a round 20 cm (8 in) × 5 cm (2 in) deep cake tin. Hold the tin with a cloth and quickly tilt to coat the base evenly with the caramel.

To make the custard

Preheat the oven to 150°C (300°F).

Lightly whisk the eggs, vanilla and sugar together in a stainless-steel bowl. Combine milk and cream in a small saucepan over a medium heat, bring to the boil then remove from the heat.

Gradually whisk the hot milk into the egg mixture. Leave the custard to rest for a minute before pouring the custard through a fine strainer over the caramel.

Place the cake tin in a deep roasting tray and add enough boiling water to come halfway up the sides of the tray. Bake for about 40 minutes or until the custard is just set; it will continue to cook and firm up as it cools. Remove from the water and set aside to stand for several hours to cool to room temperature.

To serve, run a knife around the edge of the custard, place the serving dish on top and flip it over.

STAPLE

RECIPES

BASIC STOCK (FOR CHICKEN, VEAL, BEEF OR GAME)

MAKES 2 LITRES (68 FL OZ/8 CUPS)

FOR CHICKEN:
2 chicken carcasses, chopped into medium-sized pieces
6 chicken wings, chopped into 4 pieces each

FOR BEEF:
1.5 kg (3 lb 5 oz) beef bones

FOR VEAL:
1.5 kg (3 lb 5 oz) veal bones

FOR GAME (SEE ALSO GAME TEA, PAGE 175):
1.5 kg (3 lb 5 oz) duck carcass bones, chopped into medium-sized pieces
1 kg (2 lb 3 oz) venison bones, chopped into medium-sized pieces

4 tablespoons olive oil
1 large onion, halved, skin on
1 large carrot, roughly chopped
1 celery stalk, roughly chopped
4 garlic cloves, crushed
3 tablespoons tomato paste (concentrated purée)
4 litres (135 fl oz) water

Preheat oven to 200°C (390°F). Place the carcasses or bones for your chosen stock type in a roasting tray and rub with 2 tablespoons of the olive oil. Roast for 40 minutes, turning the pieces every 10–15 minutes so they caramelise evenly all over. Once well caramelised, remove from the oven and set aside.

Heat the remaining oil in a pot or very large saucepan over a medium heat. Add the onion, carrot and celery, and cook for 10 minutes, stirring frequently. Add the garlic and tomato paste and cook for a further 8 minutes. Add the roasted bones and scrape in any of the crispy roasted pieces from the bottom of the roasting tray.

Add water, then cover the pot with a lid and bring to the boil. Reduce heat to low and bring to a gentle simmer. Cook for 4 hours, making sure to skim off any impurities that come to the surface. After this time the liquid will have reduced by half. Remove from the heat and let the stock cool slightly.

Strain the stock through a fine sieve into a container that holds 2 litres. The stock will keep refrigerated for 1 week.

VEGETABLE STOCK

MAKES 2 LITRES (68 FL OZ/8 CUPS)

500 g (1 lb 2 oz) button mushrooms, chopped into medium-sized pieces
4 tablespoons olive oil
1 large brown onion, halved, skin on
1 large carrot, roughly chopped
1 celery stalk, roughly chopped
4 cloves garlic, crushed
3 tablespoons tomato paste (concentrated purée)
2 bay leaves
2 sprigs rosemary
½ bunch thyme
4 litres (135 fl oz) water

Preheat oven to 200°C (390°F). Place mushrooms in a large roasting tray, drizzle with 2 tablespoons of the olive oil and toss to combine. Roast for 30 minutes, turning the pieces every 10–15 minutes so they caramelise evenly all over. Once well caramelised, remove from the oven and set aside.

Add the remaining olive oil to a large stock pot and bring the pot to a medium heat. Add the onion, carrot and celery and cook for 10 minutes, stirring frequently. Add the garlic and tomato paste and cook for a further 8 minutes. Add the roasted mushrooms, bay leaves, rosemary and thyme to the pot.

Add water, then cover the stock pot with a lid and bring to the boil, then remove the lid and turn the heat down low, so the water reaches a very gentle simmer. Continue to simmer for 4 hours, making sure to skim off any impurities that come to the surface. After this time the liquid will have reduced by half. Remove from the heat and let the stock cool slightly.

Strain the stock through a fine sieve into a container that holds 2 litres. The stock will keep refrigerated for 1 week.

MAYONNAISE

MAKES APPROX. 300 ML (10 FL OZ)

1 egg yolk
1 tablespoon dijon mustard
1 tablespoon white wine vinegar
250 ml (8½ fl oz/1 cup) grapeseed oil
salt
1 tablespoon lemon juice

Transfer the egg yolk, mustard and white wine vinegar to
a bowl and blend with a stick blender fitted with the whisk
attachment. Slowly stream in the oil while whisking on high
speed until the mixture thickens. Season to taste with salt
and the lemon juice.

Aioli

To make aioli, follow the recipe for mayonnaise, but first
pound 2 cloves of garlic and a pinch of salt into a fine
paste using a mortar and pestle, then add to the bowl
along with the egg yolk, mustard and vinegar.

RANCH DRESSING

MAKES APPROX. 300 ML (10 FL OZ)

150 ml (5 fl oz) buttermilk
20 ml (¾ fl oz) rice vinegar
6 g (¼ oz) garlic powder
60 ml (2 fl oz/¼ cup) extra-virgin olive oil
75 g (2¾ oz) mayonnaise
pinch of salt and ground black pepper
2 teaspoons chopped dill
1 teaspoon chopped chives

Combine the buttermilk, rice vinegar and garlic powder
in a large bowl. Whisk vigorously until the mixture is thick
and emulsified. Slowly add the oil, continuing to whisk until
combined. Add the remaining ingredients and fold them
through using a spatula or large spoon until just combined
(take care not to overwork the mixture). The ranch
dressing can be kept in your fridge for up to 1 month.

DIJON MUSTARD

MAKES 4 LITRES (135 FL OZ)

We like to think of this recipe as being one you make
in a big batch about once a year or so. This gives the
flavours enough time to really mature. Each time
you make a new batch, add some of the leftovers of
your previous batch, which will help your mustard
develop a unique flavour profile.

875 g (1 lb 15 oz) yellow mustard seeds, ground
500 g (1 lb 2 oz) honey
500 ml (17 fl oz/2 cups) apple-cider vinegar
85 g (3 oz) jarred prepared horseradish
50 g (1¾ oz) salt
80 g (2½ oz) garlic, peeled
grated zest of 5 lemons
875 g (21½ fl oz) dijon mustard from previous batch
    (or shop-bought if first batch)
630 ml (21½ fl oz) grapeseed oil
330 ml (11 fl oz) water

Add all ingredients, except the oil and water, to a blender
and process slowly on low speed for 10 minutes. Increase
the speed to medium and slowly stream in the oil through
the opening in the lid of blender. After all the oil has been
incorporated, slowly stream in water and blend for a
further 10 minutes.

Check consistency and seasoning. You are looking for a
smooth texture with no lumps or graininess. The mix may
need more blending to reach the desired consistency.

Transfer the mustard to an airtight container and store
in the fridge. The mustard will mature and become
better over time. We recommend waiting at least 1 month
after making it, but if you can wait 3 months, it will be
even better.

BUTTER

MAKES 250 G (9 OZ)

500 ml (17 fl oz/2 cups) pouring (whipping) cream

Put cream in a food processor and process for around 10 minutes, until the cream splits and solids start to form. Once the solids start to ball up inside the machine, turn it off.

Line a fine strainer with muslin cloth (cheesecloth) and set it over a small bowl to catch the liquid. Pour the contents of the food processor into the muslin, then gather up the muslin and squeeze out any liquid remaining in the solids. Place the butter back into the strainer set over the bowl. Transfer the butter to the fridge for about 3 hours so the butter sets and continues to drain.

Once set, remove butter from the muslin. It is ready to use straight away and will keep refrigerated, wrapped in greaseproof paper, for 1 week.

BUTTERMILK

If you are not making a heap of homemade butter, you can make buttermilk instead by souring milk.

MAKES 250 ML (8½ FL OZ/1 CUP)

250 ml (8½ fl oz/1 cup) milk
1 tablespoon (25 ml/¾ fl oz) lemon juice

Lightly whisk together the milk and lemon juice in a medium-sized bowl. Cover and place in the fridge to sour for approximately 4 hours before it's ready to use.

It will keep refrigerated for 1 week.

CLARIFIED BUTTER

MAKES 200 ML (7 FL OZ)

250 g (8½ oz) butter

Heat the butter in a medium saucepan over a low heat for about 10–15 minutes until melted, but not foaming, skimming any solids off the surface. Remove from the heat.

The water will have separated from the fat and be sitting on the bottom of the saucepan, so using a spoon or small ladle, transfer the clarified butter solids to an airtight container. It will keep refrigerated for up to 1 month.

CRÈME FRAÎCHE

MAKES 500 G (1 LB 2 OZ)

500 ml (17 fl oz/2 cups) thick (heavy) cream
100 ml (3½ fl oz) buttermilk

Lightly whisk together the cream and buttermilk in a medium-sized stainless-steel bowl.

Divide the mixture between two sterilised 250 ml (8½ fl oz/ 1 cup) jars. Set the jars in a warm place in your kitchen covered with a clean tea (dish) towel. The temperature needs to be around 18–22°C (64–71°F), which is an average/warm household temperature.

Set aside at room temperature for 24 hours before placing the jars into the fridge. Leave to chill for at least 3 hours before using. It will keep refrigerated for 1 week.

YOGHURT

MAKES 500 ML (17 FL OZ/2 CUPS)

500 ml (17 fl oz/2 cups) milk
1 tablespoon of cultured yoghurt (or reserve a tablespoon from your last batch)

Heat the milk in a medium saucepan over a medium heat until the temperature reaches 82°C (180°F).

Remove from heat and let it cool to 43°C (109°F), then whisk in the yoghurt and transfer into sterilised glass jars. Cover with a clean tea (dish) towel and leave to stand for 12–14 hours.

Seal the jars and leave to chill in the fridge for at least 3 hours before using. It will keep refrigerated for up to 1 week.

GLOSSARY

Aleppo pepper
Named after the Syrian city, Aleppo pepper is usually sold crushed and is characterised by its mild heat, glossy red colour and a flavour profile that marries fruity sweet with zippy tanginess. In Turkey, the predominant global producer, it is known as pul biber.

Banana peppers
Skewing palest green to bright yellow in colour, banana peppers are slightly sweet and tangy and have only the barest hint of spice to them, if any at all. They are often pickled, stuffed or served raw.

Barberries
Barberries are commonly used in Middle Eastern and Central Asian cuisines to add a tangy, acidic flavour to dishes. They are similar to cranberries or sour cherries. Barberries are rich in vitamins C and K, and also contain antioxidants and other beneficial compounds.

Black garlic
Black garlic is the result of ageing whole bulbs of garlic for several weeks until they deepen in colour and flavour. The result mellows the bite of raw garlic, lending it a sweeter, almost caramelised character. The technique originates in East Asia where black garlic has been used for centuries.

Black rice vinegar
Black rice vinegar is a type of vinegar made from black glutinous rice that is commonly used in Chinese and Southeast Asian cuisine. It has a mild, slightly sweet flavour and a deep, rich colour.

Bouquet garni
From the French 'garnished bouquet'; a bundle of fresh herbs, such as parsley, thyme and bay leaf, or other green herbs that are tied together with twine and added to soups, stews, and other slow-cooked dishes to infuse with flavour.

Brachetto wine
Brachetto d'Acqui wine is a sweet, sparkling red wine that comes from the Piedmont region of Italy. It is made from the Brachetto grape and has a fruity and floral flavour with notes of strawberry and raspberry. Good substitutes include low-alcohol red vermouth, Lambrusco or sparkling shiraz.

Calvados
Calvados is a premium French apple brandy produced in the Normandy region. It is a versatile gourmet ingredient used in both sweet and savoury dishes, adding a distinct apple flavour and complexity.

Cartouche
A cartouche is a handy lid made out of baking paper that is used to help simmering dishes reduce down gently and evenly. Rather than using a metal lid, a cartouche keeps ingredients submerged in liquid, while allowing only a little of it to gently evaporate. To make a to-size circular cartouche, cut off a square of baking paper that is larger than the opening of your chosen cooking vessel. Fold it in half and in half again. Starting from a corner tip, fold over and over into a long slim triangle. To measure to size, place the apex of the triangle at the very centre of your dish and snip off the end where it meets the edge.

Caul fat
The thin, netted membrane used to encase sausages and cured meats.

Chanterelles
Ranging sunshine yellow, orange, and pale pink in colour, chanterelle mushrooms, also known as girolles, are fragrant wild mushrooms that are gently woody in flavour, with a hint of fruity sweetness.

Cipollini onions
Cipollini onions are small, flat and slightly sweet onions with a distinctive flattened shape. They have a delicate flavour and caramelise well.

Dried Mexican chillies
Dried Mexican chillies are commonly used in cooking to add flavour, heat and complexity to dishes. They can be rehydrated (soaked), ground or toasted before use, and are used in sauces, marinades, stews and many other dishes in Mexican cuisine.

- Ancho chillies are dried poblano peppers that add a rich, smoky and slightly sweet flavour to dishes.

- Guajillo chillies are a mild and tangy dried Mexican chilli pepper.

- Chipotle morita chillies are a smoked and dried jalapeño pepper with a medium heat level and a rich, smoky flavour.

Espelette pepper
Espelette pepper, also known as Piment d'Espelette, is a mildly spicy pepper variety from the Basque region of France. It is commonly used to add flavour and heat to dishes instead of black pepper, particularly in French cuisine.

Fennel pollen
Fennel pollen is a spice made from the tiny yellow flowers of the fennel plant. It has a sweet, licorice-like flavour. Fennel pollen is highly aromatic and flavourful, and is considered a gourmet ingredient. It can be used in both sweet and savoury dishes, and is often used as a finishing spice or garnish.

Hog casings
Hog casings are the small diameter intestines of pigs used in sausage making. They are carefully sourced and prepared by butchers for their strength, consistency and ability to hold various sausage fillings. These casings are a critical component in crafting good-quality sausages.

Kombu
Dried, edible kelp that is cultivated in Korea and Japan, Kombu is usually sold in large sheets.

Lovage

Lovage is a perennial herb that is similar both in its appearance and in flavour to celery. The leaves can be used similarly to other soft green herbs, in pestos and salads, or the leaves and their stalks may be sautéed and served in the style of green vegetables.

Mustard greens

Mustard greens (also known as gai choy) are the edible leaves of the mustard plant (Brassica juncea). As their name suggests, mustard leaves are peppery and slightly bitter in flavour. The young leaves can be eaten raw as salad leaves, while the mature leaves are extremely versatile and can be stir-fried, braised and added to soups and stews.

'Nduja

Hailing from Calabria, Italy, 'nduja is spicy, cured and spreadable sausage that can be eaten on bread or enjoyed cooked. Once heated, it renders down into a moreish pairing of richly flavoured chilli oil and caramelised sausage meat.

Pastis

Pastis is a strong (to qualify as pastis it must have an ABV of 40% or higher), anise-flavoured aperitif typical of the South of France. It is usually served topped with ice water at which point it takes on a cloudy, milky hue.

Pine syrup

Pine syrup (also known as pine cone syrup or mugolio) is a sweet, treacle-coloured syrup extracted from young pine cones from the dwarf variety, mugo. Sweet and herbaceous with notes of dark caramel, it is often paired with cheese in Italy. We like Primitivizia Mugolio.

Rock sugar

Less intense than granulated sugar, crystal-like rock sugar adds a rich, yet balanced, sweetness to savoury dishes and helps to add sheen to sauces and glazes. It's commonly found at Asian supermarkets.

Salsify

Salsify is a thick-skinned, slender root vegetable available in autumn. Related to parsnip, it is similarly creamy and lends itself to hearty dishes.

Saltbush

Saltbush is a hardy, native Australian plant that can survive in desert plains and dry 'salty' plains. Used in cooking, it imparts salinity and herbaceousness to dishes. The leaves can be fried and used as a crispy topping, dried and used as a rub for meat, or blanched and used in salads.

Saltpetre

Also known as saltpeter or curing salt, saltpetre is the powdered form of the preservative potassium nitrate, used to preserve meat by preventing mould and bacteria. It's used in the manufacturing of products such as smallgoods and charcuterie.

While it may be considered a controversial ingredient by some (due to the debate around whether nitrate or nitrite is good for you), nitrate does naturally occur in everyday foods such as celery, cabbage, silverbeet and kale.

You can buy saltpetre from quality butchers or you can substitute with celery seed extract, which is available to buy from health food stores or pharmacies.

Sorrel

Sorrel is a leafy green herb with a tangy, lemony flavour that is commonly used in salads, sauces and soups.

Suet

Suet is a type of fat that has been used in cooking for centuries, especially in British and European cuisine. Suet is obtained from the hard fat that surrounds the kidneys and loins of cows and sheep. It is a solid, white substance that is very high in saturated fats.

Suet is used in cooking for several reasons. First, it has a very high melting point, which makes it ideal for use in dishes that require a long cooking time.

We like to use suet in our pastry for meat pies. The high fat content of suet helps to create a crisp and flaky crust that holds its shape and does not become soggy.

Tropea onions

Tropea onions are a sweet red onion variety that is named after the town of Tropea in Calabria, Italy, where they are commonly grown. This small to medium-sized Italian onion adds complexity and beauty to any dish, raw or cooked.

Vialone nano rice

Vialone nano is medium-grain rice variety that originates from lowlands of Veneto, Italy. It is perfect for risotto – during cooking, its high starch levels provide the dish with its signature creaminess, while its low water absorption allows the grains to hold their shape and retain some firmness.

Xanthan gum

Xanthan gum is a plant-based thickening agent used in gourmet cooking as a stabiliser, emulsifier and texturiser. It is commonly added to sauces, dressings and desserts to improve their texture and mouthfeel. Xanthan gum is gluten-free and vegan-friendly, making it a popular ingredient in modern cuisine.

INDEX

ACKNOWLEDGEMENTS

Thank you to my wife, Brittney, and our two girls, Marlow and Juno.

Thank you for supporting the long hours, early mornings, the highs, and lows. For your honesty and eye for detail, and for keeping me on the right path.

Thank you, Andrew, and Jo, for your unwavering support, mentorship and friendship. For helping to build something special that services our local and wider community, I will be forever grateful for the trust and confidence placed in me to work alongside you.

– Troy

To my wife, Jo, and my family for your unconditional love and support - you are everything.

To Troy, in many ways this is your book. Without you there would be no Meatsmith.

Everyone knows you as 'the butcher', I hope that through this book they will also come to know, as I do, for your incredible affinity with food, your love of cooking for others and your creativity.

– Andrew

TO OUR MEATSMITH COMMUNITY

To every single staff member, past and present, you have been a part of the evolution of Meatsmith and have made a huge contribution to our success and helped shape us into who we are today. To all our suppliers and producers, thank you for your dedication to growing and producing the best products our country has to offer, we are privileged to work with you and purvey your products to our community.

To our customers, we wouldn't be here without your support, thank you for inspiring us and helping us grow with you, we look forward to many more years of delicious food together.

THE BOOK

This cookbook has been a little pipe dream for a few years. It's a true expression of how we like to cook and entertain for our friends and family. We are so thrilled to have had the opportunity to publish our first cookbook together and to collaborate with such a talented group of peers, friends, and industry leaders to bring it all together.

To Chris Watson, your work ethic and taco wizardry are second to none.

To the Meatsmith team led by Dave Roberts, Sascha Randle and Aaron Starling, thank you for your invaluable input – we could not have produced this book without it.

To Chris Handel, whose capable, steady steering of the ship makes passion projects such as these possible.

To Anna Augustine, for being the sounding board and the driving force keeping everything on track. Thank you for going above and beyond and for all your help bringing this book together.

To be sure, JP makes the best colcannon. Thanks for the recipe, John Paul.

To Cam Parish, for making sense of our cocktail musings and for testing them with us – it's a tough job but there's no one else we'd rather do it with.

To Samy Mir-Beghin, thank you for sharing your steak tartare recipe, no one else helms the trolley or preparation like you do. You've made it beyond iconic, and we'll always come to you for the best tartare in town.

Thank you to our friend Josh Murphy the mustard baron and incredibly talented chef.

To Leanne Altmann. A woman of so many talents of which Meatsmith has been the benefactor since its inception. We sleep easier knowing your fastidious eye has interrogated these pages.

To our recipe testers – Emma Warren who put the more technical recipes through their paces, and our always willing in-house food lovers Dougie, Issy and Claudia who enthusiastically tackled the rest.

To the creative team, Daniel New, Mark Roper and Lee Blaylock, thank you for executing our vision so beautifully. It has been a pleasure working with you.

To Michael Harden, whose writing and editing effortlessly brought the text together – your good humour and way with words is always greatly appreciated.

And to our agent Clare Forster and the team at Hardie Grant – Michael Harry, Ruby Goss and Pru Engel for your incredible work, from the big picture to the smallest of details – we're very proud of what we have created together.

– Troy and Andrew

Published in 2023 by Hardie Grant Books, an imprint of Hardie Grant Publishing

Hardie Grant Books (Melbourne)
Wurundjeri Country
Building 1, 658 Church Street
Richmond, Victoria 3121

Hardie Grant Books (London)
5th & 6th Floors
52–54 Southwark Street
London SE1 1UN

hardiegrant.com/books

Hardie Grant acknowledges the Traditional Owners of the Country on which we work,
the Wurundjeri People of the Kulin Nation and the Gadigal People of the Eora Nation, and
recognises their continuing connection to the land, waters and culture. We pay our respects
to their Elders past and present.

A catalogue record for this
book is available from the
National Library of Australia

Meatsmith
ISBN 978 1 74379 902 4

10 9 8 7 6 5 4 3 2 1

Publisher: Michael Harry
Project Editor: Ruby Goss
Editor: Pru Engel
Design Manager: Kristin Thomas
Designer: Daniel New
Typesetter: Hannah Schubert
Writer: Michael Harden
Photographer: Mark Roper
Stylist: Lee Blaylock
Production Manager: Todd Rechner
Production Coordinator: Jessica Harvie

Colour reproduction by Splitting Image Colour Studio
Printed in China by Leo Paper Products LTD.

The paper this book is printed on is from FSC®-certified forests and other sources.
FSC® promotes environmentally responsible, socially beneficial and economically viable
management of the world's forests.